GEEKPRIEST

D1365284

GEEKPRIEST

Confessions
of a
New Media Pioneer

Fr. Roderick Vonhögen

SERVANT
BOOKS

PUBLISHED BY FRANCISCAN MEDIA
Cincinnati, Ohio

Cover design by Kathleen Lynch, Black Kat Design
Book design by Mark Sullivan

LIBRARY OF CONGRESS CATALOGING-IN-PUBLICATION DATA
Vonhogen, Roderick.
  Geekpriest : confessions of a new media missionary / Fr. Roderick Vonhogen.
    pages cm
  Summary: "In this engrossing collection of stories and anecdotes, Fr. Roderick shares how he became a "new media missionary." Focusing on the importance of personal connection (an essential ingredient of new media), he uncovers the exciting possibilities of using all forms of media to successfully accomplish the mission Jesus gave us: to evangelize the world. Each chapter contains illustrations of using new media as a way to reach out to others. Fr. Roderick›s stories introduce a young, secularized generation to an experience of God at work in his Church and in individual lives. Instead of presenting dry theories and principles, this book reveals those principles through experiences of one of today›s leading Catholic new media entrepreneurs"— Provided by publisher.
  Includes bibliographical references and index.
  ISBN 978-1-61636-676-6 (pbk.)
  1. Mass media in missionary work. 2. Vonhogen, Roderick. 3. Mass media—Biography. 4. Catholic Church—Clergy—Biography. 5. Catholic Church—Missions. I. Title.
  BV2082.M3V66 2013
  269'.2—dc23
                                                          2013018825

ISBN 978-1-61636-676-6

Published by Servant Books, an imprint of Franciscan Media.
28 W. Liberty St.
Cincinnati, OH 45202
www.FranciscanMedia.org

Printed in the United States of America
Printed on acid-free paper
13 14 15 16 17 5 4 3 2 1

CONTENTS

• • •

• • •

CHAPTER ONE

The *Star Wars* Years

Darth Vader and the Priest

The group of Stormtroopers in white battle armor was heading in my direction. So was Darth Vader, their leader. His boots splashed in the mud, and rain glistened on his helmet. They were all engaged in a lively conversation.

"Do you think George Lucas is here?"

"No, I think they said he wouldn't come. I spotted Anthony Daniels, though; he was busy cheering up those waiting in the rain."

"Why is he here? I mean, C-3PO is just an animatronic at this stage."

"Yeah, but he did the voice."

"Ah, makes sense. By the way, when do we take our first break? I need to get warm—this rain is seeping into my costume."

Darth Vader shook his head. "Jim, don't be such a wuss. You are supposed to be a Stormtrooper."

"I know. I just wish they would let us into the main tent for the opening ceremony."

I looked at the long line waiting at the former Air Force base near the Wings Over the Rockies Air and Space Museum. More than twenty thousand fans had gathered in Denver for the first ever Star Wars Celebration, just three weeks before the long-awaited premiere of the new *Star Wars* movie, *Episode I: The*

Phantom Menace. It was a cold week at the end of April 1999, and the area was experiencing the worst rain in almost a hundred years. But hardly anyone seemed to care: This was one of the most anticipated fan events of the decade. What made it unique was that Lucasfilm not only endorsed this convention—it had organized it. The movie industry had begun to discover the marketing power of fan buzz around a movie. The more fans were excited about it, the more likely they would talk about it on the Internet, thereby promoting the movie for free. This Star Wars Celebration was the ultimate way to capitalize on the excitement of the fans and to attract the attention of the media.

I looked at the program schedule I had picked up from one of the tables in the food tent. It was wet with rain and had an oily patch from the cheese nachos someone must have had for breakfast. Today a lot of the new actors were going to make their first public appearance. Among them were Jake Lloyd, who played young Anakin Skywalker, and Ray Park, a British martial arts specialist who played the red-skinned, devilish looking Darth Maul, a villain scarier than Darth Vader. Down at the museum, R2-D2 was posing for pictures underneath a giant life-size model of an X-wing, and later that day we would get to see brand new footage of the new movie. It was the ultimate liturgy for all these pilgrims wearing brown Jedi robes or "Han Solo Shot First" T-shirts who had journeyed to Denver to celebrate their common passion. Even though I shared that passion, I felt a little out of place. After all, as a young priest from the Netherlands with a Roman collar, I wasn't really following the unwritten dress code for the event. So what was I doing there?

Star Wars *Kid*

I was nine years old when I saw the first *Star Wars* movie. Since our small Dutch village didn't have a movie theater, my mom took me and my brother by train to the city of The Hague. The movie was playing in one of those old-fashioned theaters with red velvet curtains and classic movie posters of *Casablanca* and *Citizen Kane* decorating the hallways. Unbeknownst to us, the film we were about to see would become a classic movie in itself.

It was an overwhelming experience. The music, the droids, the lightsabers, and the dogfights in space were unlike anything I had ever seen. Even though I didn't understand all the dialogue because I couldn't read the Dutch subtitles fast enough at that age, the main story was easy to follow. The man in the black helmet was the bad guy, while the sympathetic boy from Tatooine who longed to be a Jedi was the hero I wanted to emulate. And of course, I instantly fell in love with Princess Leia, who was as beautiful as she was strong-willed and courageous.

It wasn't the very first movie I saw in a theater, though. That was *Jesus Christ Superstar*, the movie version of Andrew Lloyd Webber's popular rock-opera, loosely based on the Gospel accounts of the last week of Jesus's life. Up to that moment, I had only known Jesus from the stories in my children's Bible and from the big painting of the crucifixion hanging on the wall behind the tabernacle in church. But the movie made it all come alive. It featured a blue-eyed Jesus with an amazing singing voice and rather clueless apostles who probably met him at Woodstock. Nevertheless, to this young altar boy, the Jesus from the movies was a true superstar, and I couldn't understand why the evil Pharisees in their black costumes hated him so much.

But despite how much I liked Jesus and his singing hippie apostles, *Star Wars* caused them to be temporarily outmatched by Luke Skywalker and his rebel friends. Sure, Jesus could walk on water, multiply bread, and heal the sick, but *Star Wars* had lightsabers, droids, and a cool starship called the *Millennium Falcon*. And action figures! It was a story that transported me in my imagination to an exciting galaxy where life was cool, and everybody could be a hero. So different from my life on planet Earth.

I grew up in a Catholic family with a younger brother and sister in a small town in the western part of the Netherlands. Beyond the village, there was just green grass, cows, and the occasional farm building in the distance. This part of the country used to be covered in water, but thanks to the clever use of dikes and windmills, the Dutch had made it suitable for farming and habitation. During spring and summer, tourists from all over the world would marvel at this unique landscape with its tulips, grazing cows, and sheep. But to me, there was no place as boring as Holland. Wherever you went, you could always see the horizon. There were no mountains, dark forests, or mysterious caves like the ones we explored on our vacations in France. In Holland, everything was flat. And green. And predictable.

Perhaps that's why *Star Wars* made such an impression on me. I just knew how Luke Skywalker felt on his sandy home planet of Tatooine. His life at the moisture farm of his uncle and aunt didn't seem to matter. Nothing ever happened. Every season was the same as the season before. When he walked outside to watch the setting of the two suns, I hoped along with him that one day, I would be able to leave the rural surroundings of my youth and trade them for a life of discovery and adventure. In the movie,

Luke Skywalker discovered his true calling: to be a Jedi, to dedicate his life to the protection of the universe. And in the process, he saved a princess, blew up the Death Star, and hung out with a smuggler, a Wookiee, and two funny droids. It made me wonder about my own future. What was going to be my calling in life?

While most kids were playing soccer, I enrolled in a martial arts class at the age of ten. To me, it was the closest you could get to being a Jedi. I got to wear a cool white uniform that wasn't unlike the outfit of farm boys on Tatooine, and I learned how to defend myself using clever tricks instead of brute force. And just like the Jedi, I started off as an apprentice, and with the aid of a teacher, progressed through different stages, receiving a different colored belt to indicate my rank. At home, I pretended that the plastic sword I got on my birthday was a lightsaber, and the bathroom a perilous trash compactor on the Death Star.

I dreamed of becoming a comic book artist, an astronaut, a movie director, an astronomer, or an explorer. I wanted my life to be special, to mean something. Luke Skywalker embodied the kind of person I wanted to become: I wanted to dedicate my life to a cause that mattered—traveling beyond the boundaries of my own small world, learning about the mysteries of life, saving people from evil.

God probably already had an idea where this was going. I didn't have a clue yet.

Use the Force

My room was plastered with posters of star nebulas, science fiction movies, and space shuttles. After school, my brother and I would replay the adventures of Luke, Leia, and Han Solo with our toys. We used LEGO blocks to build Imperial spaceships and rebel strongholds, and Luke Skywalker fought side-by-side with Obi-Wan Kenobi to defeat the relentless army of our sister's Barbie dolls controlled by Darth Vader's powerful Dark Force.

One day, the intergalactic battle taking place on the floor of my brother's room was interrupted by my father. He looked concerned.

"Come into the living room," he said. "There is something you must see on TV!"

We followed our father to the black-and-white television in our living room. A reporter on St. Peter's Square told us that Pope John Paul I had died in his sleep. We were in shock. A little more than a month before, this friendly looking Italian man had been waving at the crowds after his election, and we were struck by how much he looked like our parish priest we liked so much. He had the same inviting smile, a good sense of humor, and always a twinkle in his eyes. And now he was dead.

That night, I thought about how Luke Skywalker must have felt when he lost Obi-Wan Kenobi. Kenobi was someone he had just met but who had quickly become a good friend and an important father figure. He died before he even had the chance to teach Luke the ways of the Force.

"What happens now?" I asked my father the next morning at breakfast.

"Now the cardinals of the world get together in the Sistine Chapel to choose a new pope," he said.

"How do they know which one to pick?"

"They will pray, and the Holy Spirit helps them."

"Oh."

I had no idea what the Sistine Chapel was or what cardinals looked like. But I liked the idea of them praying and letting the Holy Spirit provide guidance. Didn't Luke Skywalker do something similar on his approach to the Death Star when he heard Ben Kenobi's voice in his head?

"Use the Force, Luke. Let go, Luke. Trust me."

For the first time, I realized that the Church didn't operate like other human organizations—something else was going on behind the closed doors of the Sistine Chapel. It was something we couldn't see, but something we had to trust.

When the evening news finally showed us a close-up of white smoke coming from the chimney in the Vatican, we all cheered. Little did I know that the man who appeared on the balcony overlooking St. Peter's Square that evening would one day change my life completely. For ten-year-old me, however, the coolest thing this new pope from Poland did was to pick the name "John Paul II." What an awesome idea! Just like the sequel to a great movie! I liked him already.

Speaking of sequels: a couple of years later, *Star Wars* was followed by a second movie called *The Empire Strikes Back*. And by the time *Return of the Jedi* hit the theaters, our collection of action figures and other *Star Wars*-related toys had grown considerably. Even our sister now had a Princess Leia doll. The Force was strong in our family.

However, after the release of the last movie, *Star Wars* started to fade away. No more new movies, no more toys, no more new adventures. Soon, no one talked about *Star Wars* anymore. It was something of a long time ago, of a galaxy that was now far, far away.

But many years later, there was a new tremor in the Force. And I felt it.

The Return of the Jedi

"Is this thing even working?" I asked the university librarian.

"It should be. This is the fastest computer we have. It's the only one running the brand-new Windows 95 operating system."

Impatiently, I stared at the empty window of the Netscape Navigator browser.

"Perhaps other people in the library are using the Internet as well right now, so that might slow down our connection. Just keep trying."

The man walked away. It was the winter of 1996. The Internet was still a novelty for many, mobile phones looked like desk calculators with antennas, movies were distributed on VHS tapes, and nobody had heard of Google or Pixar. I had been ordained a priest a few months earlier, and I was dividing my time between my parish in the countryside and Utrecht University, where I was doing a research project about St. Thomas Aquinas.

The computer was still unsuccessfully trying to connect. The university's server was probably down. I sighed and entered the address of the search engine, Yahoo!. Back then, it was the best place to discover new content. I figured I might as well look around on the Internet while waiting for the university intranet to get back online. Out of curiosity, I did a search for *Star Wars*. To my surprise, the browser came back with dozens of websites with geeky names like TheForce.net, Jedinet, The Boba Fett Homepage, and Nerf-Herders Anonymous. My heart skipped a beat when I read the news they were reporting. It was the biggest disturbance in the Force since 1983. *Star Wars* was coming back to theaters!

George Lucas had dusted off his old notebooks and announced that he was preparing a new movie trilogy. This time the story wouldn't be about Luke and Leia but about the rise and the fall of their father, Anakin. Because the story would precede the movies he had already made, Lucas called the new movies prequels instead of sequels, and preparations were already in full swing.

When I drove home to my parish that evening, I played John Williams's famous *Star Wars* theme from a CD at maximum volume on my car stereo. I was eager to share the big news with someone, anyone really. But who? When I turned off the music and stepped out of my car on the driveway in front of the rectory, I was struck by the silence that engulfed me. The only thing I could hear was the rustling of the leaves in the trees next to my church and a few ducks in the small river on the other side of the street. I realized then that probably none of my parishioners cared about *Star Wars*. And why should they?

My parish was a small Catholic enclave surrounded by Protestant villages, and my parishioners consisted mostly of dairy farmers and their families. The contrast with my years in seminary couldn't be bigger. For ten years, I had studied at big universities in Belgium and in the Netherlands. I loved the energy of the cities I lived in—the people, the culture, and the academic environment. Now, I found myself in this very quiet town in the middle of nowhere, and the view outside my window looked just like the world from my younger years with green meadows that stretched all the way to the horizon. No shops, no movie theaters, no post office or bookstores. The only symbolic link to the outside world in which I used to live was a lone telephone booth in front of the church. My bulky old second-hand television could only receive two channels—there was no cable television available in a small town like this.

It felt like I was back on Tatooine.

But now that I knew about the existence of all those *Star Wars* websites and their thriving fan communities, I needed to do something about this involuntary isolation. I just had to get an Internet connection so I could be part of that bigger universe out there again! It is hard to imagine in the hyper-connected world we live in today, but in those days, almost no one had the Internet at home. You had to pay a hefty fee to be able to connect to the World Wide Web via a modem and a telephone line, but to me it was worth it.

A few weeks later, I had my own personal Internet connection. Finally, I could travel the planet with a few mouse clicks, I was able to participate in online discussions, and I could connect with people from all over the world. Bit by bit, my work as a priest started to expand beyond the frontiers of my parish, beyond the boundaries of my diocese.

During the day, I was a simple parish priest, celebrating Mass, accompanying the sick, burying the dead, baptizing children, or riding around on a bicycle to visit parishioners. But at night, you could find me in my pajamas sitting in front of my computer screen, typing away on my keyboard and writing articles for my website that would be read by tens of thousands of people. The topic of my website? Well, *Star Wars*, of course.

Faith and the Force

The Internet was abuzz with rumors and speculation about the plot of the upcoming prequels. Harry Knowles's website, Ain't-It-Cool News, was one of the places where thousands of *Star*

Wars fans could read the latest rumors. Hundreds of people were involved in the production of these new movies, and despite the tight security on the set, bits and pieces of information would leak onto the Internet and make their way to one of the many fan websites.

The more I read those rumors, the more intrigued I was. I knew that, somehow, the new movies about the life of Luke and Leia's father should lead to the events in the existing trilogy. Would it be possible to patch the pieces of the puzzle together and figure out the story despite all the secrecy and security? And what if I could enlist the help of the worldwide fan community in this quest for the secrets of *Star Wars*? So I created a simple, hand-coded website on which I shared my thoughts on the new movies and solicited feedback. I notified Yahoo! and soon my website was proudly listed among the other big *Star Wars* fan sites. And the number of visitors started to grow.

After a while, I felt that writing alone was not enough. After all, a movie is above all a visual experience. What would these rumored scenes look like? I needed illustrations! I taught myself Photoshop and spent many hours each week creating computer graphics to visualize the rumored scenes. A fan of the website helped me to create 3-D computer models of racing pods and spaceships that might feature in the upcoming movie, and the forum on my site became a meeting place of digital sleuths, all helping me to combine the rumors and the leaked information. From an outlet for my own creative passion, the site evolved into a thriving community of people who bonded with each other, thanks to a shared interest and a common language.

As a priest, I was not just interested in writing about the rumors or the blurry spy images from the set of *The Phantom Menace*. I had always been fascinated by the original inspiration for the *Star Wars* saga as well. In an interview with Bill Moyers, published in *Time* magazine in 1999, George Lucas said that he wanted to create a modern mythology with classical motifs to teach a young generation about good and evil. He admitted having borrowed many themes and elements from various different religions to forge them into a modern fairy tale. By introducing a mysterious energy that would help the protagonists on their journey, Lucas wanted to awaken a certain kind of spirituality in young people. It isn't by accident that Jedi wear monastic robes and live a celibate life. Just like monks and priests, they remind the universe of its spiritual dimension. When Obi-Wan Kenobi says good-bye to Luke Skywalker in the first *Star Wars* movie *A New Hope*, he tells him "The Force will be with you, always." The words echo familiar liturgical language straight from the *Roman Missal*: "The Lord be with you."

The use of universal themes present in various religions and mythologies probably explains the global success of *Star Wars*: People from all over the world could relate to elements of the story because they evoked similar themes in their own cultural and religious backgrounds. From the rumors I was gathering on my website, I could tell that Lucas did the same in the prequels. The more I uncovered about the story of the prequels, the more religious and biblical themes I recognized. Let me share a few of them with you:

• Just like Jesus, who entered the desert for forty days before he started his public ministry, we meet young Anakin Skywalker on a remote desert planet right before the start of his journey to becoming a Jedi. Coincidentally, we will meet Luke Skywalker on the same planet before he discovers his calling.

• Through a couple of wise Jedi who came from the stars and ended up on Tatooine, we discover that there is more to this child than meets the eye, not unlike the epiphany that happened when wise men from the East discovered Jesus after following the star.

• Jesus's birth was foretold in prophecies about a coming savior. In *Star Wars,* the Jedi have heard a prophecy about "the chosen one," a savior who will bring balance to the Force.

• The Jedi believe the prophecies point to Anakin who, just like Jesus, was conceived by his mother without a human father. Anakin is a child of the Force, not unlike the child of Bethlehem who was conceived through the power of the Holy Spirit.

• Soon after this discovery, Anakin has to flee from evil Darth Maul, an event that evokes Jesus's flight to Egypt soon after his birth.

• Much later, Anakin will be tested in a confrontation with an almost diabolical evil emperor. The temptations are similar to the ones the devil presented to Jesus at the end of his stay in the desert: designed to gain power by forsaking love. The evil emperor lures Anakin into believing that he can save others by giving in to the power of the dark side of the Force and by grabbing control of the Force instead of surrendering to its guidance.

• Where Anakin fails and succumbs to the temptation of power and violence, his son succeeds: Many years later, Luke Skywalker will resist the same temptations of the emperor and will bring his father back to the light by preferring to die rather than to fall for evil. The story parallels the relationship between the original Adam, who fell for the temptations of the devil, and the new Adam, Jesus, the Son of Man, who gave his life to redeem mankind.

• In the Gospel, Jesus surrenders himself to his Father on the cross, and in return, his Father raises him from the dead on the morning of the resurrection. In *Star Wars*, the father saves his son from death: When the emperor is about to kill Luke, Darth Vader picks him up and throws him into the depths of a shaft so that his son might live.

I bet you can tell that George Lucas had a Bible nearby when he came up with his story.

Even though I loved writing about these religious parallels between the two big stories that dominated my youth, I wanted my readers to know that I wasn't trying to use *Star Wars* as a tool to promote a religious agenda. I was first and foremost a *Star Wars* fan just like them, but with my background as a theologian and priest, I was able to shed light on the religious elements that may have inspired Lucas in writing the story. From the feedback I received, my readers appreciated this approach.

The website continued to grow and expand. Soon, thousands of visitors were flocking to my website on a daily basis. I started to receive tons of e-mail from all over the world with questions and suggestions from fellow *Star Wars* fans. I was invited to join TheForce.net, a website founded in 1995 by Scott Chitwood and Darin Smith, two former roommates at Texas A&M University. In a few years' time, TheForce.net had become the biggest *Star Wars* fan website in the world. It was quite surreal that my small website, created by a priest in one of the tiniest villages in Holland, could have such a worldwide reach.

But its true impact only became fully clear to me during that *Star Wars* celebration in rainy Denver.

Unusual Parishioners

We had just been admitted to the big white tent for the opening ceremony of the Star Wars Celebration when I heard someone calling my name.

"Fr. Roderick, over here!"

I turned around and saw a big guy in a *Star Wars* T-shirt waving enthusiastically at me. I had no idea who he was. He gave me a big hug that squeezed the air from my lungs.

"I'm Rob, and I can't tell you how excited I am to finally meet you," he said before introducing me to his family. "Kids, this is Fr. Roderick from Holland!"

His eight-year-old son, wearing a brown Jedi costume, and his daughter, in a white dress with a Princess Leia hairdo, smiled at me timidly.

"H-how exactly do you know me?" I asked, slightly confused.

"Dude. You're kidding me, right? Your website has been my favorite destination on the web for the past two years! I love how you tried to piece together the rumors about the new *Star Wars* film. And your Photoshop illustrations were awesome! Lucasfilm should have hired you, you know. You made everyone so excited about the new movie!"

Thanks to the added exposure after joining TheForce.net, the number of daily visitors to my website increased to tens of thousands in the months leading up to the premiere of *The Phantom Menace*. And yet, it was still a shock to discover that some of those website visitors were actually there with me in Denver that day.

"You realize that it was you who brought our family back to the Church, right?" Rob told me.

"How?" I asked.

"When our kids discovered that you were a real priest as well as a *Star Wars* fan, they wanted to go to Sunday Mass again. We hadn't been to church for years. Our local parish priest wasn't into *Star Wars*, but he was a nice guy, and little by little we became part of the parish community again. And it all started with your *Star Wars* website!"

That day, I met a lot of people who knew me as "that *Star Wars* priest from the Netherlands." Even Dan Madsen, the organizer of the Celebration, and Steve Sansweet, who worked closely with Lucasfilm, seemed to know all about my website.

I was walking quickly through the pouring rain to get something to eat when a big van pulled up next to me. A man lowered his window and asked, "Are you Fr. Roderick from the Netherlands?"

"Umm, yes, I am," I answered from under my umbrella.

"We are from CNN, and we read about you in *USA Today*. Would you have time for a short interview?"

This was starting to get surreal. A journalist from *USA Today* had called me on the phone just before I left for the United States to interview "the Dutch *Star Wars* priest." And now CNN wanted me in front of their camera. In that same week, I ended up being interviewed for *20/20*, *Newsweek*, the BBC, *Time* magazine, and a host of other magazines, radio shows, and television programs.

All this made me think: If a simple fan website about something as trivial as the *Star Wars* movies could reach so many people around the world, why didn't the Catholic Church use the Internet on a much broader scale? After all, its message was way more important and valuable than a simple science fiction movie.

Most parishes and dioceses, however, seemed to be uninterested in new media. I remembered some critical comments fellow priests had made about my hobby.

"A priest belongs in church, not on the Internet," one of them had written me after he heard about my website activities. "You could have spent all the time you invested in creating that website in prayer. Much more fitting for a priest." Criticism like that hurt because I was convinced that I wasn't doing this just as a hobby—it was a way to be present as a priest in a world beyond the confines of my parish.

Even my own bishop was skeptical. "I don't believe that the Internet can ever replace normal human contact," he once told me. "These virtual connections are dehumanizing. People stare at computer screens instead of talking to each other. It's like trying to kiss someone through a windowpane. It doesn't work."

I had great respect for my bishop, but in this case, I didn't agree. The friendships I had formed over the Internet were anything but "virtual." Even though I had never met the other members of TheForce.net before, the moment we connected face-to-face in Denver, it felt like we had been friends forever! And my unexpected encounter with Rob had taught me something else: that unbeknownst to me, God had used my silly hobby as a way to reach an entire family and bring it back to his Church. There was nothing virtual about that. I told myself that I would try to promote the Church's use of the Internet even more once I got back home.

After all, in my parish, I would reach about a hundred and fifty people in church on Sunday, but thanks to the Internet and a shared passion for something beyond Latin and liturgy, I was able to reach out to many thousands of *Star Wars* fans. Most of them probably would have never been in contact with a priest otherwise. In a way, just like the people back home in Holland, these Stormtroopers, Jedi, rebel pilots, bounty hunters, and Twi'leks had become my parishioners—very unusual parishioners indeed.

How to Speak Wookiee

When I have to prepare a homily, I always try to place myself in the position of those I'll be talking to. What are the issues they deal with, and how can the Gospel help them in their daily lives? For communication to work, you need to speak the same language. If you want to communicate with a Wookiee, you need to learn how to speak Wookiee.

So, what if you find yourself sitting next to a Wookiee on the bus and you want to start a conversation? Or what if you, as a Wookiee, are sitting in that same bus next to a Catholic who is on his way to church? What do you talk about? How can you find common ground? Here are some talking points that can help you break the silence:

• If you are a Catholic, ask the Wookiee about the prophecy concerning the chosen one, and ask if it points to Anakin or to Luke Skywalker. What were the signs that one of them truly was the one who would bring balance to the Force? If you are the Wookiee, ask about the prophecies in the Old Testament that made people believe Jesus was the promised savior.

• Ask the Wookiee about the life of a Jedi. How does one become one, and why does the Jedi Code require Jedi to stay celibate? As a Wookiee, you might wonder about the consecrated life and about priests. What makes someone give up the prospect of marrying and having children to live a life of service to the Church? Why is that important?

• Talk with the Wookiee about the Force. Ask him if he believes that everything can be explained by coincidence and biological laws and midi-chlorians, or whether he believes that the Force is bigger than that. As a Wookie, ask the Catholic what he knows about the Holy Spirit and how Catholics would react to agnostics like Han Solo or skeptics like Admiral Motti. How do Catholics deal with those who show a disturbing lack of faith when it comes to what they call "hokey religion" or "sad devotions?"

• Ask the Wookiee if he thinks the dark side of the Force is equal in strength to the light side. If you are covered in brown fur and your home planet is Kashyyyk, discuss the concept of evil, and ask the Catholic if Satan is just as powerful as God—or if it just seems that way to some.

• Finally, bring up the topic of Emperor Palpatine and Darth Vader. Ask the Wookiee what ultimately led to Vader's conversion and Palpatine's demise. What was it that ultimately saved the galaxy? If you are the Wookiee, ask the Catholic how someone's death on a cross could save mankind and be what ultimately saves the world.

• If after all that, you still haven't reached your destination, and you want to get really philosophical, ask the Catholic the question almost everyone struggles with from time to time: If God is all powerful and loving, why is there still suffering and injustice in the world, even after Jesus's death and resurrection? Ask the Wookiee why there is so much suffering in the universe while the Force is supposed to be so powerful. Why doesn't it balance itself? What causes all these painful tremors and disturbances in the Force?

No matter on how many levels Wookiees and humans differ, I guarantee you that these discussion topics will make the time go by faster than any game of Holochess. Just be careful that nobody's arm gets ripped off.

Important final tip for Wookies: When saying good-bye to a Catholic, say "May the Lord be with you" instead of "May the Force be with you."

Important final tip for Catholics: When the discussion heats up, never call the Wookiee a "fuzzball" or a "walking carpet." It's disrespectful, even if he looks like one. Always let the Wookiee win.

Things *Star Wars* Taught Me

Learning how to speak Wookiee wasn't the only thing I learned from this whole experience. A lot of the communication principles I discovered during those *Star Wars* years still guide much of what I do in new media today. Let me summarize the most important lessons learned:

Find common ground. I was able to reach tens of thousands of people from all over the world because I shared a common interest for anything and everything *Star Wars*. This enabled me to reach out to people unfamiliar with faith and the Catholic culture. The friendship that builds on this common interest can become the foundation for an exchange about other things as well, including faith. But it's not possible to get there without finding common ground first. Some Christians try to protect and solidify their identity by adopting a hostile attitude toward modern culture. I personally think an open attitude is more fruitful: Seek to find stories, values, and ideals that are compatible with your own beliefs, and try to connect with popular culture. Be *in* the world, even if you are not *of* the world.

Always start with your passion. Through my *Star Wars* website, I was able to combine two of my biggest passions: *Star Wars* and faith. It is easy to share with others what you are passionate about, and it is likely to cause a spark that might impact others. When you start with your passion, you find the energy you need to keep communicating about it. Never start a website, a blog, a podcast, or any project out of obligation or because you think there will be a market for it. Always start with something you are passionate about, and try to share your enthusiasm in what you do.

Be visual. My visitor numbers started to soar once I started to include pictures with my website articles. We live in a very visual world. The Catholic Church has always filled its churches with frescoes, paintings, stained-glass windows, and statues to visualize the stories that inspire the faithful. Why then are so many Church websites and publications predominantly text-based? A picture can say more than a thousand words. So make sure that your articles, blog posts, flyers, and bulletins contain pictures! This is even true for things like homilies or speeches; don't just communicate ideas and theories. Use stories, examples, descriptions, anecdotes—anything that can help your listeners form a mental image they can remember and associate with your message.

Create value. On my *Star Wars* website, I didn't merely repeat information that other websites published as well; I tried to create new content. Explaining the deeper layers of the *Star Wars* saga, making the connections with Bible stories, and combining all that with a quest to unlock the secret story of the new movies was something no one else was doing. Always try to create value for the audience you want to reach. Adopt an attitude of service— your audience is not there for you; you are there for your audience. Whether you write a blog, manage a business, or run a parish, always ask yourself what value you can offer to the people around you. Give people what they are looking for, and they will come back.

Make sure people can find you. One of the first things I did was register my *Star Wars* website with the big search engines of the time. It's not enough to offer value and speak the language of your audience: Your audience also needs to know you are there! Even though this couldn't sound more obvious, it is something that's often forgotten. "Why doesn't my podcast have more listeners? Why can't I reach more people with my blog? Why doesn't the young generation go to church anymore?" If you feel you are doing all the right things, perhaps you are just forgetting to get the word out about what you have to offer! If people have no idea you exist or have a message for them that is relevant to their lives, they will never connect with you. So market, advertise, make flyers, do interviews, invite, and connect!

Give people a reason to come back. It's one thing to attract people to your website, blog, business, or church. It's another thing to keep them coming back for more. *The Empire Strikes Back* ended on a cliff-hanger: Han Solo was frozen in carbonite and taken away by Boba Fett, while Luke Skywalker barely escaped Darth Vader after discovering a terrible secret about the Dark Sith Lord. Of course, everyone wanted to know how the story would end, so we all came back for more when *Return of the Jedi* was released.

In building connections via new media, you want to do the same thing: Give people a reason to come back. I could have posted all my thoughts on *Star Wars* and faith in one lengthy article. Instead, I posted bits and pieces on a daily basis so that many visitors came back the next day to see what was new. A blog or parish website that doesn't get updated on a regular basis loses its capacity to attract new people, let alone help create a community around its content.

Involve your audience. One of the ways to ensure that people come back for more is to involve them in the process of creating content. I asked my readers how they thought Lucas would tell the story of the new *Star Wars* movies. I created a forum where everyone could join the discussion, and I incorporated the best ideas in my articles. This gave visitors a sense of ownership of the website. This was not just my website—it was the result of a communal effort.

Be consistent with your updates. Every time I wasn't able to find time to post an update on my website, I would get questions about when the next article would appear. Once you establish a certain expectation, you have to make sure you meet it. People are creatures of habit. If suddenly you stop updating your blog or podcast for an extended time, your audience will drift away. As much as possible, be dependable and consistent. Find a publication frequency that works for you, and stick to it.

Share feedback. I received lots of e-mail from visitors to my site with ideas and questions. Since I was maintaining the website by hand, I didn't have a built-in commenting system like modern blogging systems now have. But even though I wasn't always able to answer each e-mail personally, I did make an effort to share the feedback I received. It gave my visitors the feeling that my site wasn't just a one-way communication—their questions and e-mails mattered, even if they didn't receive a personal reply. This is very important in institutional situations as well. Many diocesan and parish websites purposely remove the possibility of leaving feedback. Sometimes this might be a matter of prudence—not wanting to expose anyone to rude or inappropriate comments. However, not acknowledging feedback at all is a mistake. How cool would it be, for instance, if a local bishop selected a few readers' questions and answered them in a personal article, or perhaps even in a video?

Make connections. One of the best decisions I made during my *Star Wars* years was to join the TheForce.net team and add my website to their list. Some *Star Wars* websites tried to compete for visitors and saw each other as rivals, but I preferred to team up with fellow webmasters and create as much cross-promotion as possible. In order to get your message out to the world, you need others, so invest in building a network of like-minded content producers. If you have a blog about a specific topic, find other blogs similar to yours and reach out to them. Be gracious and generous toward others; treat them as friends and colleagues, never as rivals. Chances are they will return the favor!

Be personable. I always wrote my *Star Wars* blogs as if I were talking to my readers personally. I mentioned the names of people who helped me and shared personal photos of my trips to the *Star Wars* convention in Denver and Skywalker Ranch. Even today, I try to keep an informal, personal style in what I write or in the podcasts and videos I record. Your personality is what makes your content stand out from the crowd. Being personable lowers the threshold for people you want to connect with, and it facilitates friendship and a sense of community around your content. I advise my fellow priests to keep that in mind when they prepare their homilies. I encourage them to talk to their parishioners the same way they would talk to their best friends. After all, isn't that what Jesus did when he called his disciples friends instead of servants?

Have fun! Collaborating and sharing with *Star Wars* fans from all over the world was a lot of fun. Strangely enough, that's exactly why some colleagues were critical of my online activities. As a priest, I was supposed to be conducting more serious business instead of geeking out about pod races and double-bladed lightsabers. It just wasn't fitting for a priest, according to my critics. But if sharing joy and having a good time is a mistake, why did Jesus turn water into wine at the wedding in Cana? Wouldn't he have done the opposite instead?

Communication works best when your audience can tell that you love what you do. Don't take yourself too seriously, and dare to be lighthearted from time to time. It won't affect your message negatively—quite the contrary. Look how often humor is used in commercials. Think of the end of *Return of the Jedi*. Would you have preferred a long, philosophical monologue by Luke Skywalker about the dangers of the dark side to the joyful celebrations after the defeat of the Empire? If so, you seriously should consider trying out the light side of the Force. You'll have a lot more fun!

CHAPTER TWO

Spider-Man's Day Job

Saints and Superheroes

"Marvel or DC?"

"DC. You?"

"DC as well."

After this somewhat enigmatic exchange, both men smiled and shook hands. The three of us were standing in the comic book section of a bookstore in Conyers, Georgia.

"I knew right away that you had to be a DC guy when I saw you picked up Frank Miller's *Dark Knight Returns*," said the man on the left while pointing at the comic book in the other man's hand.

"Oh, this isn't for me; it's for Fr. Roderick here. He's a priest from the Netherlands, and he needs some basic education when it comes to superhero comics. He thought Spider-Man was part of the Justice League."

"Whoa. That's serious. I assume you also want to show him *Kingdom Come*. Lots of religious themes in that one. So...what do you think of the DC reboot?"

The men continued their discussion about the merits of the two big superhero publishers while I browsed through the staggering amount of comic books stacked on the shelves in front of me. I recognized a few names of characters like Wonder Woman, Superman, and Batman, or—on the shelves with Marvel comics—Spider-Man, the Incredible Hulk, and the X-Men, but most of these superheroes were new to me.

"So this is how non-Catholics must feel when they walk into a cathedral and see statues of hundreds of saints they've never heard of," I told Greg Willits while walking to the checkout counter with a large pile of superhero comic books in my arms. "I have some serious reading to do. I had no idea the comic book culture was this big!"

Greg Willits, a good friend and one of the first Catholic podcasters in the early days of that medium, was an expert when it came to superheroes. He had been reading those comics since his youth, and during my stay in the United States for a Catholic New Media conference, he had patiently been trying to teach me the basics of the genre. I however, grew up in Europe, where superhero comics don't have the same popularity as in North America. Most of my knowledge came from recent movies that featured Thor, Captain America, the Hulk, Batman, or the Avengers.

There were two exceptions: Superman and Spider-Man. These two superheroes had their own comics in the Netherlands, and I used to buy them at the bookstore with the small weekly allowance my parents gave me.

I had been fascinated by Superman ever since I saw the movie with Christopher Reeve when I was ten years old. It contained all the iconic superhero elements: a story that explained where the superpowers came from, a secret identity that allowed him to live a relatively normal life, a villain who disturbs the status quo and puts the fate of the world in jeopardy, a love story that creates the emotional attachment that drives the hero when his love interest is in danger, an Achilles' heel in the form of Kryptonite that almost seems to defeat the superhero, and a happy ending where the world returns to normal to await the next villain or extraterrestrial catastrophe.

Spider-Man was a different type of superhero. He received his powers almost by accident when young Peter Parker was bitten by a radioactive spider. Even though most Spider-Man stories contain the same heroic ingredients as the Superman adventures, I could relate to him even more because of his age and because, in essence, he used to be the same kind of shy and nerdy high school kid I was myself. (However, you would never see me anywhere near spiders. I abhor them. Even the radioactive, superpower-inducing kind.)

Back then, I dreamed of becoming a comic book artist, and I spent many evenings drawing my own superhero comics at my desk. It was a messy enterprise because I insisted on drawing like the professionals: It involved paper, pencils, and lots of hard-to-wash-off black ink. But I loved drawing and making up stories of my own. What intrigued me most was the idea of having an alter ego. In normal life, both Clark Kent and Peter Parker worked in the media. Kent worked as a reporter, while Parker worked as a news photographer. Often, this is how they got wind of new disasters or villains menacing the world. After a quick wardrobe change, they were off to protect people, dressed in flashy outfits and using their amazing powers.

It was the perfect fantasy for a nerdy kid with glasses who loved to read books at the library, but who was clumsy and slow on the soccer field. If only I could have superpowers like that! Nobody would know about them, obviously. But I would surprise all my classmates, including the bullies, if one day a meteor would threaten to destroy the school; I would appear in the sky, zapping the thing with my laser vision. Of course, I would make sure the bullies would end up at the nearest police station, ice-planet, or Phantom Zone.

Superhero 101

I learned that superheroes are very much like Catholics. Let me explain.

Just like superheroes, Catholics are powered by superhuman energy. It is known as divine love, and it is available in limitless quantities to those who are open to receive it. They recharge this power through the sacraments and by freely sharing this power among themselves. The more this superhuman power is used, the more it increases.

Just like most Catholics—especially those of the consecrated type—superheroes are not motivated by a desire for earthly possessions. Only an evil superhero nemesis craves such things, and it is usually greed, hatred, or jealousy that becomes the enemy's downfall—in combination with a couple of well-placed super-punches.

Just like priests, deacons, and bishops, superheroes wear special vestments whenever they show up for action. Even though both superheroes and liturgical ministers can be seen wearing bright colors like red, green, purple, or white, the fabric and design might differ slightly: Whereas most superheroes wear brightly colored spandex bodysuits, members of the clergy prefer liturgical vestments made of velvet, linen, or wool. Oh, and they usually don't wear masks or fancy boots, either.

Catholics are part of a global community with a common identity and a common name. However, there are other groups of Christians as well that are not formally affiliated with the Catholic Church. In a similar way, superheroes are divided into several groups. Just like the various Christian communities, they have more in common than what separates them, and yet, one group of superheroes belongs to the DC universe, while the other group has sworn allegiance to Marvel. The reasons for the separation of the two groups lie in the past, and even though the fans can get very vocal about the differences between the two communities, the different leagues of superheroes themselves seem to coexist quite peacefully on the same planet.

Just like Catholics and other Christians, most superheroes fight for a common cause: the pursuit of justice and the protection of the world against giant monsters, robots, or evil supervillains. However, they usually do this with their own friends and colleagues. On very rare occasions, Marvel and DC superheroes share an ecumenical activity, which in the comic book universe is called a superhero crossover. No matter how successful these common quests are, they have yet to result in a unification of the two camps.

Most superheroes have their weakness, their Achilles' heel. For Superman, it is Kryptonite; the Green Lantern's ring might not work on certain materials; Spider-Man sometimes runs out of webbing fluid; Iron Man has shrapnel near his heart; the Hulk is often hampered by his own temper; Aquaman can't stay out of water for too long; the Flash can't run on slippery ground; and Batman is helpless without his utility belt. Catholics also have plenty of weaknesses. For a complete list, consult a nearby Bible. For an instant cure from their effects, visit a nearby confessional with sufficient remorse and the will to do better.

Superheroes often look just like normal human beings when they are not flying around beating up monsters or villains. You would hardly notice anything special about them in normal life. Peter Parker is a regular student, Clark Kent works for a newspaper, Bruce Banner is a scientist, Tony Stark is a businessman, and Bruce Wayne is your run-of-the-mill millionaire. Catholics also usually look like normal human beings. If they are not in church, they look and behave just as normally as everyone else. You might be able to spot Catholics because many of them wear a small cross or medallion or some other religious symbol, but that is not always the case. Only nuns, monks, religious brothers and sisters, priests, bishops, and the pope are always in costume; they only change clothes when they go out for a run or when they go to bed.

Many superheroes go on a retreat from time to time. Batman ponders his life in his Batcave, Superman has his Fortress of Solitude, the Avengers gather in Iron Man's Stark Tower, and the X-Men can retreat in the Xavier Institute for Higher Learning. Catholics also have similar refuges. They sometimes stay in monasteries to pray and meditate, or they spend time in churches and chapels. The pope's headquarters are in Vatican City, although during the summer holidays, he might fly to Castel Gandolfo.

Flying as in using a helicopter, silly!

Superheroes often have a logo or symbol that defines who they are. Superman wears the iconic red and yellow *S*, Batman sports the silhouette of a bat, Spider-Man's symbol is that of a spider in a web, Flash wears the symbol of a lightning bolt, and the X-men often wear a badge with the letter *X*.

Catholics also often use symbols to show their identity. Their universal symbol is that of the cross. Saints—a kind of Catholic in which God's superhuman power is much more visible than in other people—often carry special objects that help us identify them; for example, St. Peter has keys, St. Paul carries a sword, St. Agnes carries a lamb, St. Joseph holds a lily, and St. Thérèse of Lisieux has a crucifix and flowers.

Many superheroes use accessories to assist them in their fight against evil. Thor has his hammer, the Green Lantern wears his ring, Wonder Woman uses a lasso, and Captain America has his iconic shield. Catholics also have a range of items that help them in their spiritual fight against evil. A bishop has a ring and a staff to protect his flock; many Catholics own a rosary as a tool to stay focused in prayer—and then, of course, there are censers, processional crosses, the aspergillum, crucifixes, blessed medals, and scapulars.

Every superhero isn't Catholic, and every Catholic isn't necessarily a superhero, but there is more to both groups than meets the eye.

My Secret Identity

Perhaps it was my fascination with Superman's and Spider-Man's day jobs that led me to join the local school newspaper when I was fourteen. I was still drawing comics as a hobby, and the school newspaper needed a writer and an illustrator. If I couldn't have superpowers, I could at least have the same day job as Clark Kent and Peter Parker! It was the beginning of a whole new adventure. Our school publication was a rather uninspired, text-only monthly journal containing mostly interviews with teachers and information from the school board. Almost none of my classmates bothered to read it, and neither did I.

Our new board of editors had its first meeting in a tiny office between the history classroom and the toilets. Because there wasn't enough space for the five of us, I sat on the table, browsing through a pile of old editions of the newspaper.

"Do you think it will be possible to turn this around?" I asked. "To make a newspaper that every student would look forward to reading?"

"Look how boring it is now," one of the other new editors said. Just like me, he had been invited to rejuvenate the editorial board. "Hardly any pictures, pages and pages of text, and worst of all, none of it is of any interest to us students!"

"But we included some poems by students!" objected the girl who had been the editor-in-chief for the past year.

"Right. Poems. There's part of your problem," the other guy continued. "Men don't read poems, so you are already missing half of your audience."

"Well, you men should read more poems," the girl sneered. "And not just because you are forced to read them for your litera-ture class! I suppose you would like the entire newspaper to be about sports, right?"

"Well, I bet more people would be reading this rag if that were the case!"

"You know just as well as I do that the school board would never approve. Don't forget that this is a school publication!"

"Well, what if we made a list of things students really care about?" I interjected. "We could write about a whole range of things, including school-related topics, and just mix it up so that there is something for everyone."

Our brainstorming session that day lasted several hours. In the end, we decided that if we wanted to make the school newspaper a success, we needed to change a few things.

First of all, the perspective of the stories: Instead of being a one-way communication channel for the school board and the teachers, we needed content that actually related to the things that mattered to its primary audience: the students. As reporters, we would keep our ears and eyes open and listen to what our classmates were talking about. Those were the topics we wanted to write about.

Second, the format of the magazine: Instead of this dense compilation of informational articles, we needed to inject some levity, which included some entertainment. We developed a sandwich formula: just like a sandwich with multiple layers of bread, meat, condiments, and vegetables, we planned to make the newspaper more attractive by combining the boring stuff with stories, illustrations, comics, and reviews. I started to work on a monthly comic series for the middle of the magazine. The idea was to create a story with a cliff-hanger at the end of each episode, so it would be the first thing everyone wanted to read when the next issue came out.

Third, something had to be done about the layout and the cover of the newspaper. We needed to liven up the pages with illustrations and create an attractive, magazine-like cover with artwork that would invite students to pick it up. Again, I raised my hand to volunteer. I even came up with an artist's name—RoVo. In my mind, that was what professional artists were supposed to do.

Today, more than thirty years later, the same principles still work: If you want to reach an audience, you have to make sure your message is relevant to them and corresponds to what they are searching for. If you want to pass on information about your faith, which, in itself, might not appeal to the people you try to reach, you need to wrap it in an attractive package. It's what I try to do in my weekly show, *The Break*, combining movie reviews and tech discussions with questions from listeners about the Catholic faith and traditions. And finally, in order to pique people's interest, you have to make sure that the presentation of your content is attractive. I spend lots of time and effort on the artwork of my podcasts, on the layout of the website, and on the quality of the audio and video of my shows.

After the relaunch of our school newspaper, I spent many evenings drawing comics and illustrations. My hands would be covered in ink the next morning, and I often worked until late at night to make a deadline. But the immense effort paid off. Within a few months, everybody was reading the newspaper. And what made me most proud was that nobody knew about my secret identity—my alter ego as an illustrator and comic book guy. I still remember how I walked past an empty classroom where one kid was reading my comic.

"Do you like it?" I asked.

"Yes, it's cool. Too bad it is only two pages every month. I wish the stories were longer."

"Yeah, I understand. But I can't possibly draw more with all the homework I also need to do."

The boy looked at me incredulously. "You mean *you* drew this?"

"Yep—RoVo, that's me. Roderick Vonhögen."

"Dude. I imagined someone much older and...cooler. You...you look like a nerd."

Ouch. That hurt. I had hoped for another reaction to the unveiling of my secret identity. But to be honest, I really was a nerd. I was programming computer games during the weekend, reading science fiction books and assembling model airplanes instead of playing sports, and worst of all, I still was an altar boy at church every Sunday. How could I possibly fit in with other students? I told myself that Clark Kent and Peter Parker basically had the same reputation among their peers—except perhaps the altar boy part. But I was proud of what I did, and I loved this new outlet for my creativity and curiosity.

Real-Life Superpowers

Becoming a priest was something I never saw coming—at least, not in secondary school. I always thought that priests were older people with rather dull lives, going from Mass to Mass and meeting to meeting, smoking the occasional cigar while working on their homilies. That was not the kind of life I aspired to. My plans for the future included a career as a comic-book artist, a video-game designer, a reporter, or a movie director. Heck, if I hadn't been so clumsy at sports, I might have even joined the army or the navy. But a priest? Never.

And that is when Pope John Paul II entered the picture. Years before, I had seen the live transmission from the Vatican during his presentation on the balcony of St. Peter's Basilica, but after that, I didn't really follow the news from the Vatican. As a teenager, I was way too busy with my geeky hobbies to pay attention to what was going on in the Eternal City until the morning I heard on the radio that John Paul II was planning to visit my country, the Netherlands. The public outrage that followed was shocking to me.

Everywhere in the media, Pope John Paul II was attacked and ridiculed. In my own Catholic school, teachers voiced their opposition to the pope's "medieval mentality" and his "intolerant, outdated moral positions." To my surprise, most of the students, including my own classmates, agreed. According to them, John Paul II was a relic from the past and should stay away with his old-fashioned ideas. One poll showed that only 3 percent of the Dutch population would welcome a visit from the pope. It was not only John Paul II who came under fire, though. According to public opinion, bishops, priests, and orthodox Catholics were all idiots. Suddenly, being a Catholic who liked and respected the pope was controversial. Never before had I experienced the feeling of being an outcast.

"How come you still go to church?" some classmates asked.

"Why do you want to belong to an institution that clearly doesn't understand the world of today?"

"He is authoritarian, hates women, and is only looking to expand his power and his influence!"

"You have to be blind and stupid to follow a pope like that!"

It's strange that those comments didn't really depress me at the time. On the contrary—the more I heard those derogatory comments, the more my spider sense started to tingle. Something was wrong. A real debate about the papal viewpoints many people took issue with was strangely lacking. Instead, everyone seemed to repeat the same clichés and simplifications. (At least, I assumed they were clichés.) Why didn't anybody verify what Pope John Paul II really said and wrote? The whole situation made me think of Peter Parker's frustration about the way the *Daily Bugle* portrayed Spider-Man. No matter how much good he tried to do, the newspaper kept smearing him with bold headlines like "Spider-Man: Faux-Friend or Foe-Fiend?";

"Spider-Crook"; or "Super-Hero or Super-Zero?"

However, at the same time, I was well aware that I didn't know much about my faith or the position of the Catholic Church on moral issues. I actually didn't feel that my faith played any role outside my habitual Sunday activities as an altar boy. But something told me that the Catholic Church certainly wouldn't have been around for two thousand years if there had not been something more to its message. What about all those saints, writers, poets, and scientists who were Catholic? If a writer like Tolkien— whom I held in high regard after reading *The Lord of the Rings*— was Catholic, then there had to be more to the faith. My curiosity was awakened. It was time for a thorough investigation.

I scoured the local library and started reading, beginning with Church history. I devoured stories about the early centuries of the Church and the fascinating expansion of the Catholic faith to the ends of the world. I read homilies and transcripts of speeches by John Paul II, and instead of the outdated, intolerant viewpoints the media attributed to him, I discovered someone who was very pastoral, reasonable, and clear. I joined a group of young students who were studying the documents of the Second Vatican Council. The more I read, the more everything began to make sense, and things started to fall into place. There was so much coherence in the positions of the Catholic Church that I almost felt cheated that nobody had told me about all this before. I was determined that from then on, I would never hesitate to go against the current and would always examine anything before formulating a judgment about it.

Pope John Paul II's visit to the Netherlands went down as one of the worst papal visits in history. There were empty streets on the first day, protests and riots during the following days, lackluster attendance at most of the open-air events, and ongoing hyper-critical and biased media coverage. None of it seemed to faze the pope, however. Having lived under a communist regime for most of his life, I guess he knew how to relativize what happened—much more than I could at the time. When the archbishop of Utrecht told him that squatters had printed posters announcing a reward of 15,000 Dutch guilders for anyone who would kill the pope, John Paul II reportedly just frowned and replied, "Only 15,000? That's not much!"

One event I will always remember was a Mass in Utrecht, the city where I would be ordained a priest many years later. With my mother and some other parishioners, we were representing our home parish. The event was held in a huge indoor hall, and tens of thousands of people gave the pope the warm welcome he deserved. In his homily, he talked about love and friendship: how love was the only thing that could make us truly happy, and how Jesus communicates all of God's love to us when he gives himself to us in the celebration of the Eucharist, just like the apostles experienced during the Last Supper. According to John Paul II, this love could make us creative, generous, sharing, patient, calm, ready to forgive, and full of joy. When the pope lifted the conse-crated Host to show it to the crowd, it suddenly dawned on me that this had to be the secret of John Paul II's strength and calm-ness. It was God's own love, offered to us in the Body and Blood of Christ. Now I understood why the pope was unfazed by all the criticism around him: He was filled with God's love, even for those who attacked him so aggressively.

This was stronger, bigger, and more real than any comic-book superhero power. No laser vision, flight, super speed, web slinging, indestructibility, or power ring could match this divine love, of which the pope was the messenger. This love could be felt whenever John Paul II was around. What media pundits called his "natural charisma" and his "talent to play to the crowds" was, in my opinion, pure holiness. He radiated God's own love. Even years later, when he was old and sick, you could still feel it in the air whenever he was present. John Paul II became the most influential superhero in my life. But if I truly wanted to follow his example, I would need to take a few more steps.

Origin Stories

Every superhero has an origin story. Superman discovered who he truly was and what he was called to do at the Fortress of Solitude. Old records of his father revealed to him that he was from the planet Krypton and that he was called to be a protector and a savior to people in need. Peter Parker discovered his calling at a dramatic moment in his life. He refused to stop a burglar on the grounds that catching criminals was not his job. However, when his uncle was later killed by the same burglar, Peter Parker realized that he should have done something. From that moment on, the words of his late uncle defined his mission: "With great power comes great responsibility."

I felt that same responsibility now that I had discovered so much about my faith. On the last day of his visit to the Netherlands, Pope John Paul II had had an encounter with the young people in Amersfoort.

"You are the Church of tomorrow," he told them. "You can be proud of that, but you also have to feel responsible for it. Christ is counting on you, the generation who will be adults at the dawn of the third millennium. It will be your task to pass on the message of Christ."

I remember how excited I was. This pope was counting on me to do something. To pass on what I had discovered. To play a role in the future of the Church. But most of all, I was excited by the confidence and encouragement he communicated. This was someone who truly believed what he preached, someone who was convinced that, despite what anyone else said, faith in God was vital for the future of the world and for the destiny of humankind.

It was a much-needed boost for the uncertain teenager I was at the time. I had begun to realize that there was much more to my faith than I had ever suspected, but I still felt like such a beginner. During my entire youth, I had heard that faith was about breaking bread and sharing together, about caring for the poor, about being kind to one another. But a lot of those values didn't require a belief in God. So what was the difference between a good person and someone who believed in God?

First of all, I thought, *if God truly exists, if everything I hear in church is not just a metaphor or a fairy tale but reality, then I must get in touch with God.* I knew that the best way to do that was to pray. But how on earth did that work?

I had no idea how to pray, except for short prayers before and after dinner and the standard prayers at Mass. But that almost didn't count as a personal prayer because others would lead the prayer. How do I make the first contact myself? When I asked my father about it, he told me he prayed the rosary. I was genuinely surprised. I had never seen my father pray, except perhaps in church. He also gave me a booklet with the psalms that contained prayers for each morning, afternoon, and evening. I thought this was a brilliant concept because there was always something to pray, and it would match the time of day. I cleared some space in the corner where I used to put together model aircrafts and paint my miniature armies, and from that moment on, every morning and every evening, I tried to pray.

The breviary (because that's what my father gave me) provided me with some structure, which was great. However, as soon as I tried to formulate prayers myself, I was struck by very strong, existential doubts. *What if I were just making this up myself? What if I were just talking to myself and my subconscious was trying to make me less insecure by letting me believe that there was a rhyme and reason to this life? What if all the other faithful in the world had been doing the same, creating elaborate theories to feel more secure in this short life on a tiny planet, lost in the universe?*

What if it were all just my imagination?

One day, I wrote down a short prayer on a piece of paper. It went something like this: "God, if you exist, please let me know. If you don't exist, please let me know as well, so I don't waste my time praying."

God's answer came sooner than I expected.

One of the library books I stumbled upon was entitled *J'entre dans la vie: Derniers entretiens* (*St. Thérèse of Lisieux: Her Last Conversations*). I had no idea who St. Thérèse was, but once I started reading, I couldn't put the book down. This young sister in the north of France had been terminally ill, and the book contained the conversations she had with the other sisters who surrounded her. The photos in the book showed a young girl in her twenties, and the way she talked about God blew me away. She became my teacher when it came to prayer. She made it seem so simple.

The more I prayed, the more I started to feel a certain pull. It is hard to describe, but I had the distinct feeling that God wanted something from me. But what?

A while later, I heard that a youth retreat was being organized in a convent in my diocese. *Perhaps that could be an occasion to figure out what God wanted*, I thought. I signed up and spent a few days with a group of about fifteen other teenagers under the guidance of a priest and a Carmelite sister. I was excited to discover that this sister was from the same religious order as Thérèse of Lisieux.

The priest mentioned the sacrament of confession. That was new to me. The confessional in our parish church had been transformed into a storage room for buckets and brooms. I had always thought that confession had been abolished in the sixties. That evening, I asked the Carmelite sister about it.

"On the contrary," she said. "Confession has not been abolished at all. It's one of the most beautiful sacraments there is!"

"So...um...how does it work?" I asked. "Do you just tell the priest all your sins, and that's it?"

"It isn't just about listing your sins," she answered. "Confession is first and foremost an encounter with Christ. He loves you more than you know, and when you truly meet him, you start to discover what in your life stands in the way of that love. So you entrust all those obstacles to his mercy, and he takes them away."

"If that's the case, I would love to go to confession," I said. After all, I did like Jesus. I also knew that there were many things in my life that still needed to change to be able to deepen my friendship with him.

"Just go see the priest, and ask him to help you. He will guide you through it. Don't worry about a thing."

That evening, I made my first confession. The priest was friendly and listened to me with his eyes closed, as if praying. I do not recall what he said to me afterward, but I do remember vividly the moment he stretched out his hand and told me my sins had been forgiven. It was as if a ton of bricks just had been zapped to another dimension. I felt like I was walking on air—I was so light, so relieved, so incredibly happy. That night, I hardly slept. I felt overwhelmed by God's love for me. My doubts had vanished. I didn't just believe in God on an intellectual level—I sensed that I had just met him personally.

One day, I came across an advertisement for a youth pilgrimage to Lourdes, and I asked my parents if I could go. The little town in a valley surrounded by mountains in the south of France had grown into an international shrine ever since Bernadette Soubirous reported having seen the Virgin Mary on a cold February day in 1858. Every year, millions of pilgrims flock to the site of the apparitions: a shallow grotto in a rocky mountainside by the side of a river. My parents agreed, and after a long journey, I finally set foot on the immense square in front of the sanctuary. I was overwhelmed to see the large crowd. As someone who prayed and went to church on Sundays, I was used to being an exception, a rare oddity, like a snow leopard or a panda bear on the verge of extinction. But here I was surrounded by tens of thousands of young people, and faith to them seemed to be the most normal thing in the world. I was blown away.

On the last evening of the event, I decided I wanted to know once and for all what God wanted me to do. I walked over to the grotto where Bernadette had witnessed the apparitions, and I knelt down. The evening breeze was still warm after the hot summer day, and the statue of the Virgin Mary was lit by the light of hundreds of candles. Perhaps she could help me figure out what God wanted of me. I decided to stay there until I knew.

I don't know how long I had been praying, but when I opened my eyes, I saw that most of the pilgrims had gone home. It was quiet and peaceful at the grotto. I heard the chirping of crickets and the rustling of the water of the river behind me. I knew exactly what I needed to do: I would become a priest. It was crystal clear, as if I had known it all my life. With that inner certainty, I returned home.

With abundant grace comes great responsibility.

Vatican Superheroes

For months I kept my vocation a secret from everyone at school. I had told my parents, and their reaction had been cautious—even skeptical to some extent.

"How do you know that this isn't just like all these other sudden infatuations you have had?" my dad asked. "One month, it's all about *Star Wars*. A month later, you want to join the navy. Next you transform your room into an observatory with planets and model spaceships hanging from the ceiling because you aspire to be an astronaut. What makes you think that *this* is the real thing?"

To be honest, my father had a point. I didn't know if this crazy new idea was going to last, or if it would fade away after a few weeks. But the more I prayed, the more my inner certainty increased. It didn't fade away; this wasn't a craze.

"You realize that a priest has to lead a very social life, right?" my mother asked. "It involves visiting the elderly, people in hospitals, sitting in meetings, dealing with parishioners.... You just don't seem to be a fit for that kind of life. You are always in your room building model airplanes, drawing comics, or programming computer games. You would have to give up all of that."

Perhaps. But if that was what God wanted, I would gladly give it up. I knew my mother was right: I was a rather nerdy kid who didn't relate well to his peers and who loved to be alone doing creative things. I wasn't at all a natural fit for this presumed priestly vocation. But that was exactly why I was convinced that it was a true calling! I hadn't made this up myself. Never ever had I aspired to be a priest! But the pull toward the priesthood was stronger than me—I knew I had to do this. I would have to trust that God was somehow capable of changing me into the kind of person he needed me to be.

When I finally told my classmates that I planned on entering the seminary, their reactions surprised me. I had expected disdain, laughter, sarcasm. Instead, most of my classmates were very supportive of the idea. They applauded me for choosing an ideal instead of just a career.

And so I took off for the Belgian city of Louvain-la-Neuve, where I would study at the university for five years. The seminary where I lived had students and priests from all around the world: France, Poland, Spain, Congo, Brazil, and Mexico. My world became so much bigger during those years, as did my experience of the Church. After that, I returned to the Netherlands to complete my theology studies in Utrecht, where I was ordained in 1996.

One of the highlights of my seminary years was a pilgrimage to Rome. We had been invited to celebrate Mass in Pope John

Paul II's private chapel and meet him afterward. I was nervous and full of excitement. My admiration for him had only grown over the years, and now I was going to meet him in person!

That morning, we woke up very early and headed to the Vatican. The sun had just come up, and the obelisk in front of St. Peter's Basilica cast a long shadow on the dark gray cobblestones on the square. Just before we arrived at the big bronze door that would lead us to the pope's private quarters, we noticed a small man in a cassock walking in our direction. He carried a small leather suitcase, and a black beret covered his white hair.

"It's Cardinal Ratzinger!" one of my fellow students exclaimed. Joseph Ratzinger was the Cardinal-Prefect of the Congregation for the Doctrine of the Faith and said to be Pope John Paul II's right-hand man. We greeted him and introduced ourselves. When he heard we were heading for the Vatican to celebrate Mass with the pope, he kindly invited us to stop by his office afterward and pay him a visit. I was baffled. The press at home had always depicted Cardinal Ratzinger as a strict, unfriendly intellectual, nicknaming him the Vatican's Rottweiler. This man couldn't be more different. He was friendly, soft-spoken, and seemed very accessible despite his high-ranking position in the Vatican.

After the Swiss Guards admitted us, we walked down the long hallways of the Vatican. I was gazing at the ornate ceilings and almost tripped when we had to climb the marble stairs to the upper floors of the pope's quarters. We were led to a small, modern chapel. It was dark, except for a bit of light shining on the tabernacle on the main altar underneath a big crucifix. There, in the center of the room, was Pope John Paul II. He was on his knees, dressed in his white cassock, praying, seemingly oblivious to our group. We sat there for a long time, joining him in silent prayer. Every once in a while, he would sigh and bury his head in his hands. I hardly dared to breathe, afraid of disturbing the deep silence that surrounded us.

It was one of the most extraordinary moments in my life. Being there, so close to a praying pope, was unlike anything I had ever experienced. Not only was the pope there, but God was there, too—talking to him, listening to his prayers, strengthening him. Remember the Gospel passage where Jesus takes Peter, James, and John to the mountain where he was transfigured before their eyes, his clothes white as the light while he was speaking with Moses and Elijah? Remember how impressed Peter was? That's exactly how I felt.

After Mass, we gathered in the pope's library, and a little while later, he entered the room and greeted us one by one.

"Ah, from Holland!" he said when I was introduced by the president of our seminary. He shook my hand, and to my surprise continued to ask me in Dutch how I was. "Still so young!" he said while reaching for one of the rosaries in brown plastic pouches presented to him by an assistant. With a grin, he added, "Much younger than I am!" He handed me the rosary and continued to the next seminarian. It was an encounter I would never forget.

A few hours later, we gathered in the office of Cardinal Ratzinger. He was still in a meeting when we arrived, but around lunchtime he entered the room and spent almost forty-five minutes with our group of seminarians, answering our questions and telling us about his life and work in the Vatican. I was very impressed. He easily switched between Italian, French, and German, and he seemed to enjoy the conversation with us thoroughly. I became an instant fan.

Looking back, it still feels surreal that, as a young seminarian, I had the chance to personally meet John Paul II and the man who would succeed him in 2005 as Pope Benedict XVI. We all need role models to inspire us, and these two men of God became my role models for life.

Superhero Checklist

Now you know the story about my vocation to the priesthood, but there are many vocations. Everyone has one, and it's important to discover it. What can you learn from superheroes when it comes to your vocation in life? What qualities do you need to develop? What do you need to do? Here is a short checklist:

Seek solitude. Superman has his Fortress of Solitude to which he retreats to reflect upon things and to determine a course for the future. Even a superhero like him needs silence to listen to the voice of his conscience. His colleague, Batman, feels the same need. He steps away from the world and seeks the catacomb-like surroundings of his Batcave, or he climbs a skyscraper where he stares at the horizon, lost in his thoughts.

Throughout the ages, the Catholic tradition has encouraged the same thing. It originates in what Jesus himself did, staying in the desert in solitude for forty days before the start of his public ministry. Even in the midst of his busy life, Christ often sought solitude to pray. Monasteries and churches have always been silent places that help people step away from their busy lives for reflection and prayer. Before being ordained, candidates go on retreat in silence to prepare for the mission they are about to receive.

Be sure you take time for moments of solitude and meditation. We are constantly bombarded with music, information, and entertainment, but sometimes we have to seek silence in order to really be able to hear God's voice above all the noise.

Study and read. Superheroes aren't just about action; many of them take ample time to study and to read. Take Bruce Banner or Tony Stark, for example. When they are not stomping around as the Hulk or Iron Man, they dedicate time to research and experimentation. The Flash is a chemist. Some of the Fantastic Four are researchers. Superman's movies show him studying memory crystals with recordings of his home planet, Krypton. In the X-Men comics, professor Charles Xavier creates a school where his pupils can study and learn how to apply their talents for the betterment of humanity.

When you are trying to discover your vocation or calling at a certain time in your life, make sure to make time to read. For me, reading the lives of saints like St. Thérèse of Lisieux or St. Francis helped me by showing me real-life examples of a life dedicated to God. Daily Bible readings in the liturgy of the Church often help me to reflect upon actual events and choices in my life and find the right direction to take. I continue to read memoirs or biographies of creative people and entrepreneurs to find ideas and motivation for my own projects.

Discover your strengths. The seemingly endless variety of superpowers that characterize the superhero comic book world reflects the wide variety of talents given to mankind. And just like every superhero has to discover these talents and use them to serve others, we too are encouraged to acknowledge our own unique gifts. Don't bury them; put them to good use.

When I realized that I was called to be a priest, I figured I would have to give up lots of the things I loved to do: programming computers, drawing comics, watching movies, and playing video games. However, I discovered that many of my talents resurfaced in my ministry in some way. I now use my experience with computers to build blogs and implement new technology in my new media ministry; my interest in design and drawing is very useful in designing websites and creating illustrations for blogs and podcasts; and I still review plenty of movies and video games during my weekly podcasts to build bridges between popular culture and the culture of the Church.

Acknowledge your weaknesses. Even the strongest superheroes have their weaknesses. It's the first thing their opponents look for when they want their evil plans to succeed. Not acknowledging these flaws is a recipe for disaster. This is also true for us. The more realistic we are about the cracks in our own armor, the better we can prepare for potential attacks. If you acknowledge how vulnerable you are to Kryptonite, you will be extra careful to avoid getting near it.

That is why Catholics value the sacrament of confession. This sacrament helps us acknowledge our vulnerability to sin, be honest and realistic about it, and learn from our mistakes, but it also helps us grow stronger with divine grace that surpasses our own strength. "With great power comes great responsibility" also means that we take responsibility for our sins. This is not a sign of weakness but of strength, and it is an expression of hope that we can improve with God's help.

Be humble. Most superheroes aren't as cocky and self-absorbed as Iron Man's alter ego, Tony Stark. Actually, most superheroes act out of a sense of responsibility and duty. It is never about them but about the people they try to protect. And once their role as superheroes is completed, they retreat to a humble life of anonymity, their brightly colored capes tucked away until the next call for help.

It's an attitude Jesus himself asks of his followers on multiple occasions. Life is not about honor and prestige; it is about becoming a servant to others, about humility in all you do because everything you are and the talents you have received have been given to you as a gift. Finding your calling in life ultimately comes down to finding the answer to the question: "How can I help?"

Listen to your friends. Almost every superhero story shows the importance of friends and family. Superman has his parents, and his friend and colleague Lois Lane. Spider-Man learned the most important life lessons from his Uncle Ben and his Aunt May. Batman often relies on the advice of his butler, Alfred. And both the Avengers and the Justice League show that a group of friends can be much more powerful than one man or woman acting alone.

The capacity of true friendship is what makes us such unique creatures. Where would we be without friends? The Bible reveals the true origin of human friendship: a reflection of the friendship that God offers us in his Son. And just as we are called to listen to God and discern his will, so the Bible also encourages us to listen to our friends. Value the advice of your family, and ask your friends what they would do in certain situations. Listen to the advice of the Church, for it too is built on friendship and on Jesus's commandment of love for one another.

Expect trouble. A hero's journey eventually meets with resistance and defiance—not just by the usual super-robot, crime syndicate, or evil scientist but sometimes also from within the hero's own circle of friends or family. Resolve and courage will be put to the test, and only a true hero perseveres until the end.

The same happens when you pursue your calling. Even though part of the journey might be rose-colored and happy, there will be moments when you will encounter resistance and feel like giving up. From a spiritual perspective, this could be something God allows to strengthen your faith, or it could be the activity of the ultimate nemesis who tries to divert people from God: the devil himself. Remember that even Jesus faced the devil after spending forty days in the desert.

Do not be afraid. Superheroes might not fear physical harm because of their superpowers, but they often do have to face their personal fears. For example, in the 2004 movie *Spider-Man 2*, Peter Parker is so absorbed in his superhero duties that he loses his girlfriend to someone else, his schoolwork suffers due to his crime-fighting activities, and the *Daily Bugle* newspaper is portraying Spider-Man as a criminal. Peter loses his self-confidence and is overcome by the fear of losing everything he holds dear. At one point, he is diving down the side of a building to web-sling his way through the city when anxiety strikes. His powers start to fail, and he nearly plummets to his death. It is only when he starts to care again and abandons his fears that his powers return.

Fear can have the same kind of paralyzing effect on us as well. Fear comes in many forms: fear of others, fear of not meeting other people's expectations, fear of difficult challenges, fear of making choices. Jesus kept saying to his friends and followers, "Fear not!" The essence of faith is abandoning fear and beginning to trust again: trusting yourself, trusting others, trusting God. A good question to ask yourself if you are having difficulty moving forward in life is: "Is what I do or what I fail to do motivated by fear or by trust?" If it's fear, ask yourself, "What am I afraid of?" The next question you could ask is, "How can I neutralize this fear and get past what scares me?" And perhaps you should even ask yourself, "Who could help me overcome this fear?"

If we look into the mirror of our soul, we might discover that we are afraid of many more things than we would dare to admit. Spiritual growth happens when we face those fears and replace them one by one with trust.

Be faithful and persevere. In one of my favorite science-fiction parodies, *Galaxy Quest*, a couple of actors in a *Star Trek*–like television series accidentally end up in a real space battle between the friendly aliens called Thermians and an evil reptilian warlord, Sarris. The slogan of the fictitious starship captain was, "Never give up, never surrender," but once they get involved in an intergalactic conflict in real life, their faith in that slogan is put to the test multiple times. Every good superhero story has multiple stages. You hardly ever face the final fight right away. Usually, the story contains several enemies or obstacles that need to be overcome before the final confrontation happens between the villain and the hero.

It's just like in real life. None of us experience smooth sailing from point A to point B. There are moments when everything goes well, and there are moments where things grind to a halt, where you feel stuck and unable to continue. And yet, as time passes, you find new strength or inspiration, and you move forward. Perseverance is key to any pursuit of happiness or success.

"Never give up, never surrender" is one of the key admonitions of the Bible as well, simply because we are called to be similar to God himself, who never gives up on us. Think of the story of the shepherd who keeps looking for the lost sheep until he finds it. Or the story of the father who refuses to give up on his prodigal son. Perseverance builds character, and character builds hope.

Discerning your calling in life is one of the most important things you can do to find true happiness. Happiness ultimately never depends on material possessions, or even on success in life. It stems from the inner knowledge that you are who God wants you to be, that you are doing what he wants you to do.

CHAPTER THREE

Disneyland Days

Pixie Dust and Holy Water

"Once upon a time, in a land far, far away…"

When we were kids, my younger brother and I knew that those words always marked the best moment of the day. My bed was on one side of the attic; my brother's bed was on the other side—cold feet trying to warm up the cool end of the bed; the prickly fabric of the bright orange sheets; the lingering taste of toothpaste in my mouth; and our mother, reading us a bedtime story. We had a thick, dark red *Reader's Digest Book of Fairy Tale*s. It contained all the classic fairy tales and some less familiar ones, too. The stories were beautifully illustrated with bright, colorful pictures.

But I didn't need those illustrations. I would just close my eyes and imagine I was there in fairy-tale land. Sometimes I was a brave knight on a horse; other evenings I would be exploring the diamond mines of the seven dwarfs or climbing a gigantic beanstalk all the way up to a castle in the clouds. Bedtime stories were pure magic. Just like pixie dust, they could transport my brother and me to another reality in seconds. After a while, our dreams would take over and we would be fast asleep, long before the story ended.

Reading stories was also an important tradition in elementary school. Often, at the end of a day full of math, times tables, and grammar, our teacher would reward us with a chapter from one of the adventure books we all loved. Every day, I would work hard and do my best in the hopes of hearing how the daring young captain would deal with the pirates and find his way to Treasure Island.

I even took my fascination with stories to church on Sunday. As an altar boy, I would make up my own stories during our parish priest's long homilies. I played a game of association: I would focus on an object (a candle, for instance) and try to come up with a story about how this candle was related to other objects in the church—like the holy water and altar bells. Perhaps the candle had belonged to an old saint who got lost in the woods at night. I imagined how he tried to find his way back home, using the light of the candle to find the path. Maybe he would discover a stream of holy water and follow it until he stumbled upon a herd of sheep drinking from the source. The sheep would be wearing small bells around their necks. The saint then would follow the sheep to a small chapel where he lived for the rest of his life. After all, he was a saint. And to thank God for his guidance, the saint, who was also quite handy, turned the bells of the sheep into altar bells.

When I was old enough to read for myself, I would visit the library across the street from my house. I would sit there reading until closing time. I loved the stories by Jules Verne; I loved *The Wizard of Oz*. But my very favorite book was *Charlie and the Chocolate Factory* by Roald Dahl. I must have read that book and its sequel more than fifty times. I couldn't get enough of the story of young Charlie Bucket who is the only kid who survives all the tests Willy Wonka puts him through during the tour of the chocolate factory. For a long time, I couldn't unwrap a bar of chocolate without secretly hoping I would find a golden ticket myself.

At one point, the library staff gave me permission to read books for adults, simply because I had finished reading virtually all the books in the children's section. That's when I discovered a series of books that would rival my love for the chocolate factory: Tolkien's *The Hobbit* and *The Lord of the Rings* series. These stories were amazing adventures of a scope and depth that surpassed anything I had ever read before.

I have often wondered why stories have such an appeal for me. Why do we find stories in every culture, in every century, in every part of the world? I think it's because stories are unique to human beings. Dogs don't tell stories to their puppies. They don't need to; most of what they do is instinctive. But humans tell stories to convey values, ideals, and concepts that transcend our immediate needs. Just like music and art, stories can evoke beauty and truth. They can teach us lessons and allow us to experience things we would never experience in our daily lives. They can provide guidance and direction for our lives. It's no wonder that the Christian tradition is full of stories and that Jesus himself often used stories. Stories have the ability to touch not just our minds but our souls as well.

The adventures of Bilbo Baggins, the trials of Charlie Bucket, the fairy tales my mother read to my brother and me, the stories of the Bible, and even Luke Skywalker's quest to save the universe all have contributed to the way I look at the world. They transmit values to uphold and ideals to pursue. Stories present me with role models of the kind of person I want to be: brave like Bilbo, modest like Charlie, adventurous like Dorothy, a hero like Luke Skywalker, a shepherd like Jesus.

But reality isn't always like a fairy tale. Big dreams and ideals are sometimes put to the test.

Dark Clouds over Disneyland

Rain was pouring from the sky as I walked down Main Street in Disneyland Paris early one morning. I should have taken a raincoat or an umbrella with me, but for some reason, I never thought of the possibility of rain in Disneyland. In commercials and flyers, Disneyland was always sunny and bright. But that day, dark clouds were looming over Sleeping Beauty's pink castle. The cheerful music playing over the cleverly hidden speakers in the park could barely hide the sound of thunder rumbling in the distance. I ran to seek shelter underneath the balcony of one of the brightly colored souvenir stores while a family in yellow Mickey Mouse rain ponchos bravely continued to march down the street.

"Mon Dieu, quelle temps de chien!"

An elderly man stood next to me, muttering in French about the downpour.

"I am waiting for my grandson from Versailles," he continued in French, speaking more to himself than to me. "His parents must be stuck in traffic. Could we have picked a worse day to celebrate a birthday?"

"I am sorry," I said. "Must be sad for the kid to have this kind of weather on his birthday."

The man frowned and searched his pockets. "His birthday? It is my birthday!" He unfolded a big green handkerchief with which he wiped his nose. "And the parents had the bright idea to celebrate my party here. 'It will cheer you up,' they said." He sneezed. "I fail to understand why anyone would like to see fake Disney castles when the beautiful palace of Versailles is right around the corner!"

I nodded. The man suddenly noticed my priestly shirt underneath my overcoat.

"*Excusez-moi, mon Père,*" he apologized, "I did not notice you were a priest. What brings you here right after Easter? Shouldn't you be in your parish?"

"I'm here with my parents for a short vacation," I replied, even though that wasn't the only reason I was there. "Visiting Disneyland has been a dream of mine ever since I was a kid."

That last part was true. I remembered how as kids, we were glued to the television screen when we saw glimpses of Disneyland on the *Mickey Mouse Club*. It was unlike any theme park we had ever seen. In Europe at the time, most theme parks were relatively small with swings, slides, trampolines and, if you were lucky, a roller coaster. Disneyland looked truly magical by comparison, with its giant castle, spectacular rides, and Donald Duck, Mickey, and other Disney characters handing out autographs and posing for pictures. However, Disneyland was on the other side of the ocean in the United States, and as a child I never thought I would ever travel that far.

But in 1992, a European version of the park opened near the city of Paris, and after a few difficult years (with plenty of opposition from some of the French who considered it to be a hostile American takeover of their beautiful country), it soon grew into the most visited theme park in Europe. And now, I was finally there myself. However, it was not exactly because I was on a short vacation with my parents. In reality, I was on sick leave on doctor's orders, and the rain and dark clouds perfectly matched my inner state. I was unhappy in the happiest place on earth.

Chocolate Meltdown

Little more than a week earlier, right before the start of Holy Week, I had visited my doctor. I was suffering from sleeplessness, and I felt stressed and tired. Worst of all, I wasn't motivated to do anything anymore. Even my parish work, which I had loved during the first years after my ordination, had become a burden. The short visit to my physician turned into a forty-five-minute conversation. His conclusion? I was overworked and suffering from burnout. I had to stop working immediately, and if possible, try to get out of town and take a leave of absence.

My parents had planned to spend Holy Week and Easter in France that year, and when I told them the outcome of my visit to the doctor, they graciously invited me to come with them. It was a difficult decision to make. How could I relinquish my parish duties during the most important week of the year? With confessions, Holy Thursday, Good Friday, the Easter Vigil, and the other Easter Masses, I felt I couldn't leave.

"That is exactly your problem," the doctor had said. "You feel like the world is on your shoulders, and you try to be everything to everyone."

I knew he was right. I had been sent to this rural parish all by myself, with no other priest nearby to give me guidance or share the workload. Our diocese had hundreds of parishes and was short on priests, so even newly ordained priests were often assigned to remote parishes before they had time to grow into their ministry. But I was full of energy and ready to take on the job. I had been studying and preparing for this work for ten years, and I felt I could handle anything God would send my way. I would turn this small parish into a flourishing community, filling the pews with families again, and showing everyone that I was exactly the priest the world needed. Had my life been a Disney movie, I would have cast myself as a knight in shining armor with the Sword of Truth and the Shield of Virtue, always ready to help people in need.

I couldn't have been more wrong.

Initially, everything was great. I loved the interaction with my parishioners, the conversations with the sick, the dedication of many volunteers, and the beauty of celebrating Mass. I worked long hours every day, sometimes sitting through parish meetings that lasted until midnight. Parishioners knew they could always call me, day and night—and sometimes they did. If someone asked for the anointing of the sick in the middle of the night, I would jump on my bike and speed over narrow country roads to one of the farmhouses in the area to be there with the family. It was all part of the mission I had accepted during my ordination. The more I did my best to be always available, always ready to help wherever I could, the more my parishioners expected me to always be there to do exactly what they wanted me to do. But more and more, I started to notice that I couldn't always match those expectations. And soon, cracks started to appear in my shiny armor.

As a young priest in my early thirties, fresh from seminary, I noticed certain things in my parish that needed some adjustment. Just as the Prime Directive of Starfleet is not to be ignored by local starship captains without consequences, the Catholic Church also has a set of universal rules and stipulations that priests are required to obey. But some of my predecessors had been flying solo for far too long and had forgotten about some of these universal directives. I felt that it was my responsibility to try to make some necessary course corrections. However, every time I tried to implement any changes, I was overruled by the local church committees. I was told that I should just follow the local, unwritten rules that this parish was accustomed to. It caused quite a bit of internal conflict.

On one hand, I wanted to be on good terms with everyone. I wanted to be liked and appreciated. Wasn't I supposed to be a good shepherd? Always patient and friendly? Never causing tension or discord? Just going along with whatever the parish expected me to do would be the easiest and fastest way to keep everybody happy. On the other hand, I had a promise to keep. During my ordination, I had put my hands in those of the bishop.

"Do you promise respect and obedience to me and my successors?" he asked, looking me in the eye.

"I do," was my answer.

I knew my bishop wanted me to make sure that my parish was functioning in line with the universal Church. What's more, I was convinced that those rules and regulations were important to safeguard essential values and beliefs. But every time I tried to suggest change, no matter how prudently and friendly I formulated it, it seemed to provoke resistance and friction. At one point, the church council appointed a coach to help me "get organized and better understand the local customs." It was well intentioned, but I felt like I had been placed under guardianship. I had lost my freedom. I was frustrated and angry. Angry at myself, for not meeting my own expectations, angry at my parishioners for their unreasonable demands, and—to my own surprise—angry at God.

After all, how could God let this happen? Why did he send me to this parish to minister all by myself? Why couldn't he have given me parishioners who were easier to work with? Surely there had to be other, better parishes for a new priest without experience? Why did he allow all this stress? Why couldn't he have prepared me better? I had given my life to the Church, and this was what I got in return? Why did I spend ten years studying philosophy and theology? Was it so I could fight with parishioners over the right to use the official liturgical texts during Mass? This wasn't what I signed up for!

Of course, all that anger didn't resolve anything. It only made it more difficult to find the energy to do my work. And it made it difficult to pray as well. I started procrastinating, watching movies until late at night, and trying to console myself with bags of potato chips. Things were going downhill, and the more I tried to escape the pressure of all the expectations, the more the pressure grew.

One sunny day, I was driving home from a visit to the supermarket in the nearby town. The plastic crate in the back of my car was filled with bread, meat, frozen vegetables, and even a big carton of chocolate ice cream that I needed to put in the freezer as soon as possible. When I turned the corner and approached the church, I noticed an unusual number of cars parked on both sides of the road. A large group of people was gathered on the square in front of the entrance. The doors of the church were open. Strange...what were all these people doing there at this hour of the day? It was just a regular Friday. That's when I noticed the bride and groom. My heart stopped. The wedding! I forgot all about the wedding that day!

I rushed out of the car, entered the rectory, and ran into the sacristy, where the sacristan was pointing at his watch. "Where were you? We have been looking for you everywhere!" I apologized while quickly getting into my alb and chasuble. As I rushed to the church door, I realized that I didn't even remember the names of the bride and groom. How could I have forgotten something so important? During the entire wedding celebration, my heart was racing faster than that of the wedding couple. My blood pressure must have been through the roof.

When I finally waved good-bye to the newlyweds, I let out a deep sigh. *That was close.* I walked back to my car to unload my groceries, or what was left of them. I had parked my car in the sun. The ice cream had melted, and the box had started to leak. There was sticky chocolate goo everywhere. It was the perfect symbol of my own personal meltdown.

The Sword and the Apprentice

As I left the gate of Sleeping Beauty's castle, I noticed a familiar scene to the left of the small square in front of me. There was a big anvil with the heft of a sword sticking out of it—an image from the story of the *Sword in the Stone.* "Who so Pulleth Out This Sword of this Stone and Anvil, is Rightwise King Born of all England," said the inscription. I remembered watching the movie as a kid. It told the story of young Arthur, an apprentice of the powerful wizard, Merlin, who fulfilled the ancient prophecies about the new king by being the only person who could pull the sword from the stone.

The sword in Disneyland had an almost magical pull on me. Would it be possible to get it out of its socket? I had to give it a try myself. I walked up to the anvil and pulled. The sword didn't move. I pulled again with a bit more energy. Still no movement. I looked around me to make sure no one was watching these silly attempts by a grown man to remove this sword from its socket, and with two hands, I gave it one last pull. Nothing. It was completely stuck. Perhaps the sword could only be pulled out during a live performance of the tale. There probably was a release mechanism hidden inside the rock that I couldn't activate myself.

This was the perfect metaphor for my life at that point. I was stuck. How could I get out of this situation? I had tried so hard to be the priest I thought I was meant to be, but it seemed that all my attempts had been futile. Pulling myself out of this situation was clearly something I was unable to do by myself. I needed help.

When I returned from France, I did the only sensible thing I could think of: I talked with my bishop. He had heard about my sudden sick leave and showed great empathy and fatherly concern.

"There are two things I can do," he said. "I can move you to another parish, so you can make a fresh start. Perhaps I can find you a place with another priest so you can have some support.

"But," he continued, "you risk running into the same kind of problems elsewhere, too. So the other option would be to get you help to face the situation you are in and find a way to deal with it without getting sick again. It might be a lot harder, but it could make you stronger in the end."

Remember the movie *The Matrix*? Neo, the protagonist of the story, is offered the choice between a blue pill and a red pill. The blue pill would offer an easy way out, while the red pill would allow him to face the reality of the situation. One pill was an easy escape, and the other pill would lead to a possibly painful but ultimately more redeeming confrontation with reality. Guess what?

I took the red pill.

I decided to stay in the parish and ask for help. For several months, I had long talks with a counselor appointed by the diocese, and little by little, I started to discover how things had gone wrong. It wasn't God's fault. It all had to do with the knight in shining armor I expected to see in the mirror. There was an important spiritual lesson that I still had to learn: There is only one Savior of the world, and I am not him.

One of the scenes in Disney's *Fantasia* is based on Goethe's poem about the sorcerer's apprentice. Mickey Mouse finds himself in the workshop of an old sorcerer, tasked with a number of chores. Even though he is just an apprentice, he enchants a broomstick to help him carry water. But the broom is out of control, and Mickey tries to stop it by splitting it in two with an axe. The two halves develop into two separate brooms that continue to multiply and fill the room with water. When all hope seems lost, the old wizard enters, breaks the spell, and returns things to normal. Mickey learns that he isn't the master, and things can go terribly wrong when an apprentice tries to wield magic on his own.

That was the lesson I had to learn as well. In my enthusiasm and idealism, I had tried to do everything alone. Sure, I prayed, but did I really ask God what he wanted me to do? All too often, it was I who announced my plans to God, asking him to help me get it done. That's why I had never really wanted to accept and acknowledge my own boundaries and limitations. I thought I could do it alone.

Once I realized that, it was as if a huge load was lifted off my shoulders. For years, I had been trying to pull the sword from the stone by my own strength. Instead, I should have asked God to switch the lever that activated the hidden release mechanism. He should take the initiative, not me. I could only do my best; God would do the rest.

My solution to dealing with the overwhelming amount of responsibilities as a priest and the sometimes-unrealistic expectations of the people around me was acknowledging that I was only an apprentice. I wasn't called to save people; only God could do that. I wasn't called to solve each and every problem; only God could do that. And I wasn't obliged to say yes to everything that was asked of me. It was perfectly all right to say no if I thought that something was beyond my power and possibilities. After all, just like Mickey Mouse, we are only apprentices, helping the Master where we can. This was the attitude Jesus recommended to his disciples: Always remind yourself that you are just a servant, just doing what the Master asks you to do.

When I was in the middle of the storm, almost drowning in the waters I had conjured up myself, I couldn't see any positive outcome. But now that I look back at what happened, I realize how much I learned from it. I learned to discern what God really was asking me to do instead of standing in his way with my own plans. I learned to protect my boundaries and say no to what might be good in itself but not part of what I was called to do. I learned that doing my duty was good enough and I could trust God to take care of the rest.

Pinocchio's Confession

When Walt Disney adapted Carlo Collodi's story about Pinocchio into an animated movie, he greatly expanded the role of the talking cricket in the story. In the original tale, the cricket is smashed by Pinocchio after berating the puppet for his mischief and disobedience. Disney christened him Jiminy and turned the cricket into more of a companion and friend, while still retaining the idea of him being the voice of Pinocchio's conscience.

Even though I love the original, edgier version of *Pinocchio*, I admire the way Disney's version stresses the importance of Jiminy Cricket's role for the puppet's journey toward becoming a real boy. The Disney movie emphasizes the choice of whether to listen to your conscience or not. When Pinocchio refuses to take Jiminy's advice, he almost ends up as a donkey, but then he redeems himself by sacrificing his life to save Geppetto from the whale. The Blue Fairy certifies Jiminy as Pinocchio's official conscience.

This was one of the most important lessons I've had to learn over the years: to listen better to my conscience. In my early years as a priest, I often acted out of concern for what people expected of me. I said yes to anything they asked because I was afraid of the consequences of saying no. I forgot to listen to my inner voice that often told me to slow down, protect my boundaries, and not worry about people's perceptions or expectations.

Just like Pinocchio in Stromboli's puppet show, I was a people pleaser. There is nothing wrong with that in theory: Wanting to help and please people is a good thing. But it becomes a problem when it's done for the wrong reasons. Why was I ignoring the inner voice of my conscience to bend over backward to please people? Was it the fear of being judged? Of not being accepted? Of being criticized? All the while, I kept telling myself that I was doing what God wanted me to do: being a good priest, living my life for others. But I forgot to listen to what God was really asking me to do, and I started to feel like a marionette that danced on command.

Part of the process that followed my time in Disneyland was rediscovering the inner voice of my conscience. It is the echo of God's own voice, helping us to discern how to do good and avoid evil, to make the right choices. The sacrament of reconciliation was an important help to me during that time. Even for many Catholics, this sacrament is not something they are familiar with. Some associate it with fear and punishment, while others believe confession has become irrelevant because the entire concept of sin is something of the past, and guilt is a feeling that stands in the way of one's personal development. Others are under the assumption that it's enough to admit your mistakes in a private conversation with God without the presence of a priest.

But let's take another look at the story of Pinocchio. The scene where the Blue Fairy visits Pinocchio while Stromboli is being holding him prisoner in a birdcage presents us with a good metaphor for what confession truly is.

Pinocchio is a prisoner as a result of his own disobedience. The Blue Fairy appears, and Pinocchio at first is afraid and ashamed. Jiminy Cricket encourages him to come clean and tell the truth, but when the Blue Fairy asks him why he didn't go to school, he makes up lie after lie. Each time he lies, his nose grows. But after the Blue Fairy helps him see the error of his ways, he asks for forgiveness and expresses his resolve to never lie again. The Blue Fairy gives him another chance, and in the process, unlocks the cage and frees Pinocchio.

It is my experience that the personal nature of an encounter with someone from the Church who has been given the authority to forgive sins in God's name is the biggest strength of the sacrament. Just like the Blue Fairy, a priest who hears your confession is not there to instill fear or to judge you. His role is closer to that of a doctor, a healer, or an advisor.

No matter how much we pretend that we no longer suffer from sin or guilt, in reality, both are very much part of our daily lives. Pinocchio is afraid to come clean and confess because he knows very well what he did was wrong, and he feels guilty about it. The same is true for the sacrament of confession. It isn't always easy to acknowledge your sins and take an honest look at yourself. It is much more comfortable to rationalize your mistakes and not face the confrontation with a priest. But will you really be honest with yourself? Confessing your sins can help you better discern the good that you could do instead, and feelings of remorse can turn into positive resolve to change your life and become a better person—with God's help.

Just like the Blue Fairy, a priest can ask helpful questions and give you advice for the future. Having someone else look at your situation can open up perspectives you wouldn't find by yourself. The Fairy had the power to forgive Pinocchio and give him another chance after he showed true remorse and the resolve to not lie again; a priest has the authority to forgive you your sins in the name of the Father, the Son, and the Holy Spirit.

A Disney Examination of Conscience

If received regularly, the sacrament of reconciliation can help you in your spiritual growth as it informs and refines your conscience and guides you in the decisions you make on a day-to-day basis. To prepare for a confession (or to evaluate your day before you go to sleep), you can use what is called an examination of conscience. This is a list of questions or reflections that help you look at the various aspects of your life and your relationships with God and those around you.

What kind of questions should you ask yourself? You actually already know. You have been hearing these questions since you were a kid. Fairy tales and other stories are full of them. Many fairy-tale characters help us to discover which values are truly important and which dangers can block the way to our destiny to live happily ever after. So here they are in a virtual parade, meant to help you reflect upon your life by asking you a question they also asked themselves:

Jiminy Cricket: Do you try to do what is right, or do you just do what you like and what is easy?

Pinocchio: Did you always tell the truth? Have you been reliable and dependable?

Thumper: Have you always been kind to people? Did you laugh about other people or tease them without charity? Remember, "If you can't say something nice, don't say nothin' at all."

Snow White: Did you take care of the people in need around you, especially the little ones?

Prince Charming: Have you given in to fear, or did you show courage when needed?

Cinderella: Are you obedient to your parents and others in authority (even when they aren't very nice)? Do you always help cheerfully when people ask you to do a job?

The Tortoise: Were you patient enough, or did you rush through life like a hare?

Donald Duck: Have you lost your temper, or were you firm but kind?

The Three Little Pigs: Did you build your house on the rock? Is Jesus the foundation of what you build in life, or do you have too much trust in your own abilities?

Belle: Did you judge someone on the basis of how he or she looks? Did you really see the inner beauty of the people around you?

Scrooge McDuck: Did you share things with others, or were you greedy and kept everything for yourself?

The Seven Dwarfs: Did you help the homeless and the persecuted?

Hansel and Gretel: Do you eat too much at the wrong times or in a greedy manner?

Goldilocks and the Three Bears: Were you hospitable to people or did you scare them away?

The Woodsman: Have you shown mercy to others, even if it might have cost you?

Little Red Riding Hood: Are you kind to your grandparents?

The Sorcerer's Apprentice: Were you humble enough to do your duty, or did you try to find an easy way out?

Princess and the Pea: Are you always complaining about minor things, or are you able to offer things up?

Dumbo: Do you use your ears? Do you really listen to other people and to God?

Alice in Wonderland: Do you fight injustice, or do you look the other way?

Little Mermaid: Are you willing to make sacrifices for the people you love?

The Lion King: What kind of a leader have you been to others? Were you honest, brave, and humble or self-centered and ruthless like Scar?

Robin Hood: Did you give to the poor?

Tinkerbell: Have you been jealous?

Sleeping Beauty: Did you go to bed in time? Did you sleep enough, or too little, or too much?

Grumpy: Have you hurt other people through your grumpiness?

Aladdin: Did you pretend to be better, richer, or more important than you actually are?

The Genie of the Lamp: Were you helpful to other people? Have you been careful to protect your boundaries, or have you said yes to too many wishes?

Off to Neverland

"This is one of the oldest rides in the Disney theme parks, and yet it is still one of the most popular," Deborah explained while we slowly made our way through the long line of people waiting for Peter Pan's Flight. "It was one of the main attractions on Disneyland's opening day in 1955, but this one in the Magic Kingdom is an enhanced version."

I was back in the world of Disney. But this time, it wasn't in rainy France but in sunny Florida, and I was in much better spirits than the last time. Deborah, a Catholic podcaster, was my guide today. She and I cohosted a podcast series about classic Disney movies, as well as a series about the fairy tale–based TV show, *Once Upon a Time.* She knew the world of Disney's classic movies better than anyone else and had been working at the Magic Kingdom for many years.

"So what is different about this version?" I asked.

"Well, it is on a bigger scale than the one in Disneyland, and it contains Captain Hook's pirate ship."

It was one of the rides I missed years ago in Disneyland Paris. Back then it was closed for repairs because of a mechanical problem. This time, I was determined to experience it, even though a sign told us that the wait would probably be another forty-five minutes.

Peter Pan has always been one of my favorite Disney movies. The story of a couple of kids who fly over moonlit London to Neverland to beat evil Captain Hook never gets old, just like Peter Pan himself. And even though the original story by J.M. Barrie from 1911 is relatively new when compared to the stories by Hans Christian Andersen or the Brothers Grimm, *Peter Pan* still has all the characteristics of a classic fairy tale: It features an island far from our own reality; it has mermaids, fairies, and other fantastical creatures; there is a battle between good and evil; and it has a happy ending.

But the most important characteristic of fairy tales, also true of *Peter Pan*, is the element of discovery—the discovery of something that transcends the story itself. Its value can only truly be uncovered by experiencing the story. In *Sleeping Beauty*, it is the power of true love's kiss; in *Pinocchio*, it is the value of truth and honesty; in *Dumbo*, it is the awakening of self-confidence; and in *Cinderella*, it is the discovery of inner beauty and human dignity beyond class and appearances.

Peter Pan is a story about the boy who wouldn't grow up, and about Wendy, the girl who needs to grow up. After her father tells her that she is too old for fantasy stories, Peter Pan makes an appearance in her room and takes Wendy and her brothers to Neverland. When she finally wakes up again in London and tells her parents about the adventures she experienced, her father sees what looks like a pirate ship in the clouds outside the window. He suddenly remembers that same ship from a long time ago, when he was very young. This ending highlights what the adventures in Neverland lead us to discover: the value of childhood, dreams, and fantasy.

Perhaps that is why fairy tales in general have such a lasting appeal and are transmitted from one generation to the next. They allow us to undergo a process of transformation by taking us away from the reality in which we normally live to experience a story in heightened contrast that gives us certain insights. And when the story has ended, we return to our normal lives with what we have learned. Stories have an incredibly evocative power that surpasses pure theoretical discourses. The Bible is full of stories that illustrate the many facets of God's relationship with us, and Jesus often used parables to communicate important insights. The fact that we still remember them after two thousand years is proof of the power of storytelling.

In a certain way, the different forms of storytelling in our culture—whether books, movies, television shows, cartoons, comic books, or video games—mirror the function of rituals in religion. Liturgy is, in many ways, a ritualized form of storytelling as well. Every time we leave the worries of our daily lives and enter a church or a cathedral, we are transported to another world, a place where stories, songs, images, colors, and rituals all lead us to discover the hidden mystery of our world: the love of God that transcends liturgy itself and becomes something that can change the way we live in the present and give direction to the future.

In recent years, we have seen a steady rise of TV shows and movies based on classic fairy tales. The television series *Once Upon a Time* brought characters like Snow White and Prince Charming to our modern world and focused on the theme of hope that characterizes many fairy tales. *Grimm* chose another approach by using classic tales of the Brothers Grimm as inspiration for a police drama where fairy-tale monsters and villains are real. Movies like *Alice in Wonderland*; *Mirror Mirror: The Untold Adventures of Snow White*; *Snow White and the Huntsman*; *Jack the Giant Slayer*; *Maleficent*; and *Red Riding Hood* show that there continues to be a market for modernized versions of familiar fairy tales. There will always be a need to step away from reality into a different world to learn and discover what truly matters. In the pilot episode of *Once Upon a Time*, one of the characters says it very well: "What do you think stories are for? These stories, the classics…there's a reason we all know them. They're a way for us to deal with our world—a world that doesn't always make sense."

Back in line, a friendly voice reminded us in English and Spanish to always remain seated and to keep our hands and legs on the inside of the miniature galleon during the ride. A few minutes later we were flying over miniature buildings of London on our way to Neverland. In *The Story of a Soul*, St. Thérèse of Lisieux mentions a line from a poem her father taught her: "Life is your ship and not your home." When I looked down from the floating galleon, I saw a story that resembled my own life. I had been that child who dreamed of adventure, but only learned how to fly after discovering that "all it takes is faith and trust." I thought I had to grow up, to take the lead, to be in control. But over the years I had to learn to let go of that control, to let God take the lead, and to trust that he would carry me to my destination, just as this galleon seemed to navigate the skies by itself.

How do you share such an experience? How can you convey your discovery of a world that lies beyond what our eyes can see?

It's one of the most challenging tasks for a priest like me—for any believer, for that matter. The kids returning from Neverland try to convince their parents that what they experienced was real. But for someone who hasn't shared that experience, the stories are hard to believe. Perhaps that is why Jesus said to his disciples, "Come, and you will see." It is by sharing his life, by following him on his journey, that bit by bit we become believers and witnesses. This idea shaped the way I started to use new media. Thanks to a small audio recorder, I would take people along with me wherever I went: to Ireland, to China, to Greece, and even to the Vatican.

CHAPTER FOUR

Adventures in the Vatican

The Night the Pope Died

It was dark and chilly when I stepped onto the roof terrace of the Pontifical Dutch College. I looked at the city of Rome below. There was the orange glow of the streetlights, a car driving down the hill in the direction of the Circus Maximus, the echo of a dog barking somewhere in the neighborhood. There were familiar buildings, churches, and monuments. I loved this city. I used to have my room on this floor of the building. The white-tiled terrace was my favorite place to sit, read, or pray after a long day at the university. It was so quiet and peaceful. In the distance, I saw the beautifully lit dome of St. Peter's Basilica. I turned around to head back inside. That's when I heard the church bells.

Wait. Church bells? I checked my watch: it was 9:45 P.M. Why were they tolling the bells this late in the evening?

A few seconds later a second church began to toll its bells, and a third one. And then it dawned upon me. I knew what was going on. Quickly, I searched my pockets for the small digital audio recorder I had been using for interviews earlier that day, switched it on, and pointed it toward St. Peter's dome in the distance to record the moment. More and more churches were tolling their bells now. Soon, churches in the entire world would follow this example to honor the great man who had just passed away. John Paul II had died.

I rushed down the stairs and grabbed one of the bikes the Dutch priests used to go to the university. It was a rusty yellow mountain bike with hand brakes. Perfect. A few minutes later, I was racing down the hill over the cobblestones of the Via Appia toward the Vatican, pedaling as fast as I could. I was trying to steer with my left hand while recording my voice with the recorder in my right hand.

"Once the city realizes that John Paul II has passed away, a lot of people will be heading to St. Peter's Square tonight," I said into the recorder while barely evading a Vespa coming from the right. "They will want to be there to mourn this pope, to remember what he meant to them personally, what he meant to the Church and to the world. And we are going to join them there."

I had just been there an hour ago, praying with the crowd underneath the pope's window. For days, this massive, silent crowd had been gathering around the central obelisk on the square to support John Paul II in the final days of his life. I had flown in from the Netherlands a couple days earlier. I wanted the world to know what was going on, and the easiest way to share it was by recording what was happening, adding my own personal comments—not as a journalist, but from the perspective of a simple priest from a small town in a small country in Europe.

I had grown up with this pope. I remembered cheering and waving when he entered the big convention hall for Mass when he visited my country and how I just could not understand why most of the media felt the need to ridicule him. I thought back to the trepidation I felt when I met him in person during pilgrimages to Rome when I was still in seminary. I remembered his warm handshake, his encouraging words, and even his jokes about his advanced age. My connection with him had only grown stronger during my recent two-year stay in Rome as a student in social communications. I had prayed with him and listened to his teachings every week. I remembered concelebrating Mass with him during the Easter Vigil and how, despite his fatigue and frail health, he tried to give everything he had. Could anyone understand how much this man meant to me?

There was going to be plenty of news coverage about the death of John Paul II. All the big news companies had their anchors, cameras, and satellite dishes in position on the rooftops of the Via della Conciliazione. But in order to really understand what this historic event meant to a generation of Catholics and to the people of Rome, there was room for another account of the unfolding events told by a "Catholic insider."

That night, I walked around St. Peter's Square for hours. The windows of the pope's private quarters were still lit. The crowd kept growing now that the news of the pope's death had interrupted television shows and radio programs all over the world. Some young people were singing and playing guitar, while others were praying the rosary near one of the fountains. Most people were just talking quietly among themselves, reminiscing over the many years that John Paul II had been their leader and shepherd.

I tried to capture the special atmosphere by recording the sounds around me, describing what I saw, and formulating my own thoughts. Sometimes camera crews noticed my Roman collar and stopped me, and I had to answer questions in Spanish, German, Italian, or English. But most of the time, I was the one interviewing others, like the young student who tearfully told me how much John Paul II's presence at World Youth Day had affected her life.

When I returned to my room well past midnight, I uploaded the recording to the Internet and went to bed. The next day, I discovered that thousands of people had already downloaded the recording and listened to it. My inbox was overflowing with reactions. "I saw the reports on CNN first, but then I listened to your recording, and it was as if I was right there with you!" "I am not even Catholic, but I was moved to tears." "Please continue these recordings and let us know what is happening. The media here are all repeating the same information."

In the days that followed, I kept returning to the Vatican to make new recordings and post them on the Internet. On April 5, I woke up at 5:00 A.M. to stand in line for hours to pay my respects at St. Peter's Basilica. When I slowly walked past the body of this great man who had inspired me so much as a seminarian and as a priest, I realized that his death marked not only the end of an era, but also the end of an important part of my personal life. For years, I had witnessed him traveling the world to meet people and tell them about Christ. He was never afraid, and he sacrificed himself until the very end. I would never forget him.

Cappuccino in Rome

The Pontifical Gregorian University in Rome has the best cappuccino in the world. Served quickly by one of the always slightly grumpy ladies behind the counter, the white porcelain cup is filled to the brim with hot, dark coffee covered by a thick layer of steamed milk froth. A fellow Italian student told me how to test the quality of the froth: If you add a spoonful of sugar, it should rest on top of the milk and only slowly sink down to the bottom after a few seconds.

The moments of bliss while sipping my cappuccino always marked the start of long, busy days at the Interdisciplinary Center for Social Communications, located on the top floor of the centuries-old building. After my first five years working as a parish priest in the Netherlands, my bishop sent me to Rome. At first, I was going to write a dissertation about the theology of Hans Urs von Balthasar, a Swiss theologian I specialized in during my studies in the Netherlands. But soon after my arrival at "the Greg," as we students called the university, I discovered the existence of an institute that offered courses on how to make radio and television programs. Students could also take a wide range of philosophical, theological, and sociological courses in the field of communications. I remember being very intrigued by the photo of a radio studio on their brochure. Students were manipulating rows of sliders and buttons while talking into professional studio microphones. According to the brochure, there were courses on movie analysis, video production, editing, journalism, the Internet, mass communication theory, and much more. I was intrigued. I had never thought you could study such modern, high-tech subjects at this venerable university founded in 1551.

"You are most welcome to follow our curriculum, Fr. Roderick," the rector of the Institute said while handing me some papers from behind his desk. "In fact, many other students here take our courses in addition to working on a dissertation project. And it won't cost you extra since your diocese is already paying for your theology studies. You can specialize in either journalism or radio production. If you want to learn more about communication on the Internet or master television production, we offer that too."

"How much time would I have to invest?" I asked.

"Oh, not much; you can easily do it along with your existing studies."

That turned out to be a little too optimistic. The two-year curriculum was comprised of daily courses at the university as well as several hours a day of study and homework. But after the first week, I was convinced that I had found my destiny. This was exactly what I needed to study. Communications. Media. Transmitting the message of the Gospel in our modern world, using all the communications knowledge and expertise built up over the past decades.

"I am going to show you something," our teacher in a video production class told us. He switched on a monitor and pressed a button to play a video. Our class watched a television show where a priest was sitting in a chair on a darkened set, a few bookshelves and some plants in the background, being interviewed by someone sitting in a chair opposite him. They talked about theology. The image switched between the priest, the interviewer, and a wide shot of the set.

"So, who can tell me how you know that this is a Catholic video?" the teacher asked us.

"Is it because there is a priest being interviewed?" a Ugandan sister asked.

"It is Catholic because they talk about Catholic theology," suggested a student from Peru.

"I noticed some Catholic books on the bookshelves behind them," said someone else.

Our teacher shook his head. "You can instantly see that this is a Catholic video," he said, "because it is *boring!* Look at it! Just talking heads. No creativity! A set that looks like it was built in the seventies! This isn't even television. It's radio with a couple of cameras switched on!"

The teacher paced back and forth in front of the TV. "This, ladies and gentlemen, is the problem of Catholic media. It's terrible! Compare this with all the other media out there. Spielberg movies. Polished advertisements. Quality documentaries. Creative TV formats. Who is going to watch this boring stuff when there is so much better television available? Our Church has the most beautiful message in the world, but who is going to notice it if we do such a lousy job presenting our message in the media?"

He went on to explain the goal of the two-year curriculum. They would challenge us to rival the best media people out there. Whether we would specialize in journalism, radio, Internet, or television production, the Institute wanted to turn us into media professionals.

"If after these two years, you get to work at a local television company, I want you to be taken seriously and demonstrate that you can work at the same level as anyone else working there. It means these two years are going to be very intensive, and some of you might not make it all the way to the end, but our Church needs quality communicators. And you can be one of them."

Wow. I didn't expect this kind of introduction. But he was right. Wasn't communication the big bottleneck for the Catholic Church? Its message is every bit as relevant as it has been for the past two thousand years, but for some reason, we have forgotten how to communicate it well. We often don't know how to use the media, and even if we do use it, our efforts are often clumsy and lacking in quality. In addition, a lot of people who should know how to deal with the media, like bishops and priests, are often wary of or even hostile toward journalists and reporters.

"I hate newspaper journalists," a priest from my own country told me while we were talking about the media over a cup of coffee. "They always distort what you say. They constantly try to depict the Church in a bad light. So I refuse to do interviews anymore."

"But people did the same with Jesus," I replied. "That didn't stop him from preaching and communicating his message."

"Fr. Roderick, you are naive," the priest said with a sigh. "The Church should stay away from the media. They will only make things worse. I stopped watching television a long time ago. I just communicate to my own parishioners via our church bulletin. That way, at least, I am in control of my message."

I couldn't believe my ears. Of course, using the media presents certain risks: the risk of being misunderstood, the risk of being criticized or ridiculed, the risk of a journalist twisting a story to make it more sensational. But at the same time, the media presents the Church with a tremendous opportunity to reach a lot of people who would never set foot in a church. How effective is Catholic media if it is directed inward and only caters to those who are already Catholic? What about our mission to reach out to the ends of the world?

When I told my bishop about my newly discovered passion, he wholeheartedly agreed that this was what I should focus on.

"To be honest," he told me, "theology is important, but there are many theologians. This, however, is something that nobody specializes in. We need all the help we can get to communicate better, especially to young people. You have my blessing. I am convinced it is important."

Now that my bishop had confirmed my intuition, I doubled my efforts. I knew I had only two years to complete these studies, and I wanted to squeeze out every bit of information and knowledge about social communications that I could. I worked long hours every day, walked around Rome for hours with a camera on my shoulder or a radio microphone in my hand; I spent entire nights editing video footage and took every course I could possibly work into my schedule. Needless to say, soon I needed more than one cup of cappuccino to keep me going!

Five Steps for Effective Communication

One of the best decisions I made while studying social communications in Rome was signing up for a course in radio production. It wasn't the specialization I had picked for my main curriculum—I chose television production instead—but I had heard great things about the teacher: Seàn-Patrick Lovett, program director at Vatican Radio. Lovett is a dynamic, engaging teacher with a great sense of humor and a wealth of experience from the many years he worked in Vatican communications.

That one course laid the foundation for almost everything I do today in Catholic media. If I had to pick one thing he taught me, it would be the "Five *Is*" of effective communication, and I'd like to share them with you. Five steps, all starting with the letter *I*, that apply to blogging, podcasting, writing a book, making a radio or television program, or even to preparing a homily.

1. Interest. A couple of years ago, I spoke at a conference in Rome about social media and about how social networks can help us reach people outside the Church. During the coffee break, an older Italian priest walked up to me.

"I don't agree with what you said!" he told me. "You claim that Twitter and Facebook are good tools to reach young people. They are not!"

"What makes you say that?" I asked.

"Here, look at my Facebook page!"

He opened a laptop. The page looked rather empty, except for his name and a small photo of the priest, looking stern and serious into the camera.

"Read this! I wrote that if people have questions about faith and want to talk to me, they can do so. Guess what? Nobody. Nothing. *Niente.* I have been waiting for weeks, and nobody wants to talk to me! So don't tell me that Facebook is a good place to communicate. It doesn't work!"

I was so taken aback that I didn't know what to say. This priest lived under the assumption that a simple photo and one Facebook post would be enough to attract thousands of young people to his page. Unfortunately, he wasn't the only one with this attitude. In our parishes, we often behave in the same way. "Why don't people come to church anymore? We have such a great community!" No matter how important your message is, nobody will know about it unless you find ways to catch their interest.

Every day, we are bombarded by hundreds, if not thousands, of messages. The Internet brings us limitless choices of programs, videos, articles, and messages. If you want your message to stand out, it needs to be interesting—not just to you but to the people you want to reach! One way to make sure your content is of interest to others is to start by asking yourself what your target audience is looking for. What are their interests? The next thing you need to figure out is how to make people curious enough to read your blog, listen to your podcast, or watch your video.

This is where a lot of communication fails. You might have written a wonderful book, but if the title isn't appealing, or the cover looks boring, chances are people won't even pick it up and open it. The next time you are in a bookstore, take some time to study the covers of the most popular books on display. You will notice how innovative some publishers are in trying to get your attention. You can do the same thing while looking at your Twitter feed. Which tweets make you curious enough to click on a link? How are they phrased? What triggers you to look further? The more you study how others successfully capture *your* imagination, the better you will become at catching other people's interest yourself.

2. Inform. Just attracting people's interest is not enough. You need to offer content. Information. Answers to the classic questions of who, what, where, when, and why. We all have a message to convey, information we want to spread. If there is no information, your blog post, video, or podcast becomes irrelevant. Strive to provide excellent, well-researched, and well-presented information. Make sure it has value to your audience: Provide them with content they wouldn't want to have missed. If you do that on a consistent basis, people will keep coming back for more.

Again, it is worthwhile to look at your own media consumption. What are the blogs and resources that keep you coming back? We are attracted to sources of information that provide us with exactly the information we are looking for, to the point and in a concise way. That is why Wikipedia is one of the most visited websites in the world. It specializes in providing relevant information about a wealth of topics. The Vatican also puts a lot of effort into providing complete and exact information to its website visitors: News, documents, radio programs, photos, and videos are the main reasons why people visit the Vatican online. So ask yourself if your own communication provides people with information that is relevant to them.

3. Instruct. Information caters to knowledge, and instruction impacts behavior. Do you know which videos are most searched for on the Internet? Sure, cat videos. But after those? How-to videos. Instructional videos that show you how to fix your bike, how to install a hard drive, how to cook the perfect lasagna. Instruction provides people with something they can apply in their daily lives.

As communicators, we want to leave an impression on someone. We want to change people's behavior. A piano teacher wants to help students learn how to decipher musical notes and translate them into music. A television chef wants to show you how to make the perfect lasagna, so you can prepare it yourself. This desire to change people's behavior is central to religious communication as well. A priest wants to help you translate the Word of God into action. It is his task to help you understand and apply the message of the readings to the choices and behaviors in day-to-day life. If that practical application is absent, a homily might still be interesting and informative, but it will lack transformational power. Or think about the liturgical year. Year after year, times like Lent or Advent invite you to change your lifestyle and the choices you make.

4. Involve. If there is one thing the evolution of new media and social networking have taught us, it's the importance of involvement. Communication isn't a one-way street. It is an exchange of meaning, and that exchange creates community. Advertisers, radio hosts, and television personalities all do their best to involve their audiences by inviting them to participate in the program, by liking their Facebook pages, by voting in a poll, or even by creating videos or sending in snapshots. They know very well that if someone contributes to a program or a discussion around a brand, it generates a sense of ownership. People feel a stronger connection because, in a way, their contribution makes them co-owners of the message or product.

For a long time, this has been a weak point of religious communication. As a lot of it is one-way only, people don't feel involved. But slowly, the Church is changing, and the rise of social media has greatly contributed to this change. More and more priests, bishops, cardinals, and even our popes have started to reach out via social media, inviting people to react and to ask questions. This also means receiving negative feedback from time to time, but even negative reactions are a sign that people are involved. Often, if you respond politely and in a friendly manner, much of the initial negativity might become more favorable. It is easier to lash out at someone you don't know than to stay angry with someone who treats you nicely, even if you weren't nice yourself.

5. Inspire. Religious communication can't stop with the previous four points. It needs to go one step further—it needs to inspire. The word *inspire* comes from the Latin word *in-spirare*, to "breathe into." The word *spirit* in Greek and in biblical Hebrew is the same as the word for breath. What we ultimately want to communicate is the Holy Spirit itself. He is the source of all our creativity, and he wants to communicate himself to the world through us. If something inspires us, we describe it as a breath of fresh air. Ideally, that is what religious communication should bring to our audience. This is something you can't totally control or master with techniques alone. The one who inspires is the Holy Spirit, not us. The best thing you can do to be inspiring to others is to be inspired yourself, to open yourself to the workings of the Holy Spirit.

The great theologian St. Thomas Aquinas was known to pray before he began his studies, writing, or preaching, and in this prayer, he asked for light and wisdom, insight and eloquence. Every priest, before he reads the Gospel, prays that God may cleanse his heart and his lips to worthily proclaim the Gospel. I also always pray a short prayer in silence before I start my homily: that God may use me to touch the congregation through his Holy Spirit, that he may inspire those who need to be inspired. Similarly, I also try to pray every day for the people I reach through the media I'm involved in. I am not exactly sure how it works, but I am convinced that it matters.

My First Podcast

It was the morning of February 23, 2005, a couple of weeks before the death of John Paul II. Even though the sky was clear and the sun was shining, it was a cold day in Rome. I was back in the city I loved so much for an unexpected opportunity: to speak about new media at a conference organized by the Vatican. At the beginning of the year, I received a phone call from the secretary of the Pontifical Council for Communications asking me if I could come to Rome for a two-day conference on Church and Media. They had heard that I was actively developing a number of new media initiatives in my diocese in the Netherlands, and they wanted me to focus on the pastoral possibilities of new media. I was surprised and intimidated by the proposal. The thought of having to speak at a conference full of high-ranking Church officials, communication experts, publishers, and journalists scared me to death.

"Will I have to give my talk in Italian?" I asked.

"Italian, or Spanish, German, English, or French—whatever works best for you. We have live translation for all our participants because they are from all over the world."

Somehow this only made me feel more insecure. After all, who was I? I was just a simple priest from the Netherlands experimenting with some website projects for my diocese. Most of my fellow priests still thought it was just a glorified hobby. But clearly, the Vatican was taking new media a lot more seriously.

Just after Christmas, one of my parishioners sent me an e-mail asking me if I had ever heard of podcasting. Since he worked a lot with entrepreneurs in the field of new technology, he had come across an interview with a certain Adam Curry, a former MTV presenter who lived in the Netherlands. Curry was excited about a brand-new technology that allowed you to put recorded audio programs on the Internet in such a way that people could automatically download them and listen to them on a mobile device, like an iPod. Since this parishioner knew about my interest in new media, he suggested that this might be interesting to explore further.

I searched online and found Adam Curry's show, *The Daily Source Code*. When I clicked the link to the audio recording, my computer started playing something that sounded like an American radio show with jingles and a professional radio voice, but the big difference from traditional radio was the personal content of the program. Curry would talk about anything that crossed his mind; he talked at length about his day-to-day experiences, his noisy neighbor, his coffee machine, and his ideas and projects. Sometimes, he would take his digital recorder with him on a trip and record in the streets of London or Los Angeles or even in the middle of the night on a plane. Nothing was scripted, and nothing was prepared in advance. I couldn't stop listening. What I loved about this new medium was how personal it was. Even though it resembled radio, the way in which Curry was using it felt more like a personal blog. It was a refreshing change from the overproduced, scripted programs on radio and TV where the emphasis is on information and entertainment. Podcasting was about real life and real people. And of course, since these podcasts were distributed over the Internet, there were no restrictions when it came to duration or reach: Anyone on the planet with an Internet connection could download and listen to them.

When the Vatican invited me to this conference, I knew that I absolutely wanted to talk about podcasting. Most people only thought of websites and perhaps this new thing called blogging when they heard the words "new media," but I was convinced that this podcasting technology was the beginning of a media revolution. Anyone could become an audio and video producer and could potentially reach a worldwide audience. As a priest, I could too! That's why I purchased a small iPod and a digital audio recorder at the airport just before I boarded my flight to Rome. I would do exactly what Adam Curry had done: record a podcast while walking in Rome. And I would play the recording from my iPod during my talk at the conference. More specifically, I wanted one person's voice to be on the recording: John Paul II's.

On that chilly Wednesday morning in Rome, I flipped the recording switch and started walking to the metro that would take me to the Vatican. While recording the sounds of the city, I tried to describe my surroundings as well as I could. I remembered being upset when I noticed a child on the metro begging for money while his father played the accordion. "Shouldn't this kid be in school?" I asked my future listeners. Several passengers gave me puzzled looks because I was talking into this small microphone all the time. They couldn't see the invisible future audience that was traveling with me via this audio recording. (I have had a lot of puzzled looks from people around me in the years that followed, and I sometimes still get them.)

When I arrived at the Ottaviano station, I looked at my watch and started to run. I had heard that the pope was recovering from an illness and that the normal Wednesday audience on St. Peter's Square had been canceled. According to *L'Osservatore Romano*, the Vatican's newspaper, John Paul II would make an appearance at the window of his private quarters to bless the crowd at noon. My watch showed that it was 11:55. The station was still a few streets away from Vatican City, so I ran as fast as I could. I apologized to my future listeners for being so out of breath, and I told them that I wasn't sure I would arrive in time to record the pope's voice. When I finally reached the right side of the huge square, hardly able to speak anymore after all the running, I noticed that nothing was going on. I walked toward the obelisk in the center and looked up at the window of the pope's study. Closed. Had I been mistaken? I asked one of the Vatican security guards if the pope was still going to make an appearance. "No, he is not," he replied.

Great. Here I was, recording my very first podcast in order to let people share in the excitement of seeing and hearing the pope, and he didn't show up. This wasn't going to be a great demonstration material for the conference the next day, but at least it was real. This is what happened; it was not scripted—I was out of breath, disappointed, and hungry.

The next day, I headed over to the Vatican for the conference. I had formed a mental image of what the conference hall would look like: marble floors, beautifully decorated ceilings, Swiss Guards showing people to their seats. There was none of that. In reality, the conference was taking place in a state-of-the-art conference center with a projection screen, wireless headsets for the translations and comfortable, modern chairs. There was a new ceiling with spotlights—Michelangelo had never touched it. I was sitting in the third or fourth row, listening to the various speakers from Italy and other countries. My turn would be the next day, so I had time to prepare myself mentally for my presentation and get to know some of the people present. The first few presentations weren't very interesting. They were long, theoretical, and often read from notes. Fortunately, I was able to understand most of the languages used, so I didn't have to wear the headphones for the simultaneous translation that was provided.

However, I was starting to seriously doubt whether my own presentation would be a good fit with this audience. I had prepared a PowerPoint presentation, and I knew what I wanted to share, but my presentation was nothing like the large amounts of texts and bulleted lists that these first speakers were projecting on the big screen. I have a visual mind, so I like to use pictures in my presentations. I never write notes for my presentations; I prefer to walk around with a wireless microphone and talk from the top of my head. I had prepared some practical examples of interesting new media projects; however, this conference seemed to be very academic in nature.

During one of the coffee breaks, I shared my concern with one of the conference attendees. He told me not to worry: This was merely a very Italian conference, and hearing about some practical examples would actually be a refreshing change for the audience.

The biggest problem with Italian conferences is not the academic approach, though. It's the food. It is way too good, and there is too much of it. For lunch, we enjoyed a fine Italian three-course meal with pasta, a salad, and traditional *Saltimbocca alla Romana* accompanied, of course, by a good glass of wine. When we came back to the warm conference room after a walk through the cold streets of Rome, the next speaker was a French publisher with another long, academic presentation. Sleep overtook me, along with quite a few of my fellow conference members. It's always difficult to fight sleep without letting the people around you know that you are dozing off. So I leaned forward and buried my head in my hands as if I were thinking intently about the presentation that was going on and on.

I woke up to the sound of a cell phone going off. One of the journalists sitting next to me searched his pockets frantically, embarrassed that he forgot to put his phone in silent mode. A few seconds later, another phone rang somewhere behind me. The French speaker looked up and frowned before he continued his talk. Then another phone went off. And another. Even a Vatican official on the panel seated right next to the speaker picked up his phone and answered it with a look of concern on his face. Some journalists stood up and walked outside with their phones. The French publisher bravely tried to ignore this strange phenomenon, but it was clear that something had happened somewhere in the world. And then I heard the helicopter. From the sound of it, it was flying very nearby. Ever since 9/11, there was a strict no-fly zone over Vatican City, so what on earth was a helicopter doing there? Suddenly it hit me: The pope. Something was wrong with the pope. He had been ill for the past few days; the day before, he didn't show up at his window. What if...? Could he...? I didn't want to think about what might have happened. But I knew that I wanted to record what was going on. So I reached for my digital recorder and started to give a whispered account of what was happening around me.

At that moment, one of the monsignors took the microphone. "You must all have understood by now that something is going on. We have been notified that our Holy Father, Pope John Paul II, is being taken to the hospital. We don't know any other details. We will briefly interrupt our conference."

Still recording, I walked outside toward St. Peter's Square to see if I could find out more about the pope's condition. However, most people I asked had no idea what had happened and looked genuinely surprised at the news that John Paul II had been rushed to the hospital. I stumbled upon a Belgian priest who told me that the pope had been moved to the nearby Gemelli Hospital; he was heading there by taxi to do a live television report in front of the hospital. I joined him in the cab as we raced through the streets of northern Rome, still recording everything that happened.

I will never forget the view of the parking lot in front of the hospital. The entire place had been taken over by television vans and hundreds of journalists. As I followed the priest to the perimeter of the parking lot, I heard the hum of the many power generators that fed the lights, cameras, and satellite dishes of the international broadcasting companies. To do their live television reports, journalists stood side-by-side in front of an impressive line of television cameras. I heard the same story over and over again in various languages: Pope John Paul II was hospitalized after suffering a pulmonary crisis. No further details were made public at present. That was it. No other news to report. And yet, the eyes of the entire world were set on the hospital in the background, so these journalists had to keep talking. I have always been amazed at how news outlets like CNN can fill hours of live reporting when almost no news is available. When they run out of facts, speculation begins. Could this be the end for Pope John Paul II? If he were to die that night, what would happen next? Who would be his successor?

When I finally got back to the Dutch College that night, I uploaded my audio recording to the Internet. I fired off an e-mail to Adam Curry, who was in the United States at the time, to let him know that I had heard him talk about podcasting, and that I had recorded a podcast in Rome about the events that happened that day. The following morning, my e-mail inbox was swamped with reactions. Thousands of people had listened to my podcast because Curry mentioned it in his popular *Daily Source Code*. He was very excited about the personal "live on the spot" feeling of the recording—so different from conventional studio recordings or run-of-the-mill news coverage on location. What I considered to be a disadvantage—that I was just a regular priest instead of a professional radio reporter—was, in his eyes, a huge advantage.

It allowed listeners to experience the events through the eyes and ears of a Catholic insider, someone who knew the Catholic Church from within. The name for my podcast was born: *Catholic Insider*.

Vatican Podcasting

Many of the e-mails I received that day were from people who were not Catholic. And they had plenty of questions.

"Who takes over the pope's job now that he is ill?"

"Is the hospital of the pope run by nuns?"

"Can you tell us what happens when a pope dies?"

"How is life in Rome? What is your favorite restaurant?"

"Could you give us an audio tour of St. Peter's Basilica?"

I returned to the Church and the Media conference for my presentation that day. There were fewer people than the day before; most of the professional journalists had been put to work by their press agencies right away to cover the developments at Gemelli Hospital. I told the story of the podcasts I had recorded and how the immediate response had been overwhelming. I showed my brand-new iPod and summed up the advantages of this new medium compared to traditional media: Production costs were extremely low, distribution via the Internet was fast and cheap, anyone on the planet with an Internet connection could download the recordings and listen to them whenever they wanted, and most important of all: Podcasting allowed a much more personal connection with the audience, enhanced by their ability to send feedback and suggestions for future recordings.

After the conference, I walked to St. Peter's Basilica and recorded a new podcast to show my listeners around the Basilica. I wasn't sure if I was allowed to do this, but nobody seemed to pay attention to a priest whispering into a small device in his right hand.

People probably just thought I was praying. Encouraged by the big success of these early audio tours, I got the idea to pay a visit to someone I held in high esteem who I thought might be interested to hear about this new podcasting technology: my former radio teacher, Seàn-Patrick Lovett.

The offices of Vatican Radio are situated on the right side of the Via della Conciliazione, close to the open square leading to Castel Sant'Angelo. I had no idea if he would be in his office that day, let alone have time for me. After all, with the pope in the hospital, everyone involved in media and communications was undoubtedly very busy. I walked through the dark-colored glass door with the Vatican coat of arms above it and introduced myself to the receptionist. The man behind the desk made a phone call and then told me I could go upstairs; Mr. Lovett was in his office.

I walked through long corridors past countless studio doors. Some were open, while others were closed with a red ON AIR light burning next to them. In every room, I heard a different language: German, Italian, French, English, Chinese, Russian, Arabic. Vatican Radio transmits programs to five continents in thirty-nine different languages, twenty-four hours a day, seven days a week. What struck me was how many young people worked here. Presenters, editors, technicians, journalists: The place felt like a large, contemporary news agency instead of the old-fashioned baroque environment many people picture when they think of the Vatican.

I had been in this building once before when I did my final exam in radio production. In addition to a written exam, we also had to host a radio show in a real studio with a technician at our disposal. The show wouldn't be aired on Vatican Radio, of course, but everything else was as real as possible. We had to make sure that everything ran smoothly. I was nervous but still looking forward to the experience. I had planned for a morning-show type program with jingles I had mixed myself. I planned to invite listeners to call in on the topic of anger and frustration, especially when technology fails and computers break down. This topic of experiencing computer failures on a daily basis while editing was close to my heart. What I didn't know was that the whole exam was rigged. Our teacher had asked his colleagues on a different floor to actually call in during our radio show to see how we would react. I remembered how shocked I was when the technician gestured that I had an actual caller. That wasn't part of my script! To make things worse, the caller started to ask all sorts of annoying questions. Why I was playing pop music on my program. Wasn't I a priest? Shouldn't I be focusing on religious content? Did my bishop know I was on the radio? On the other side of the glass window, I could see Seàn-Patrick Lovett laughing, while I got more and more flustered by this irritating caller. When I wrapped up the session, he congratulated me for having survived the hijacking of my show. "It was a lesson to teach you that no matter how well you prepare, things always go differently from what you expect. But you stayed relatively calm. Bravo!"

When I walked into his office, Lovett greeted me enthusiastically. After I told him about podcasting, he had two questions: (1) Is it good? and (2) Is it useful? In answer to the first question, I told him about the amazing response my first few podcasts had, including responses from an audience that wasn't Catholic. As to the usefulness of this technology, I told him that I was convinced that podcasting was an amazing opportunity for Vatican Radio.

In order to reach remote countries, the Vatican relied on powerful shortwave transmitters that were very expensive and ultimately only delivered a weak, low-quality signal to the listener. However, with podcasting, audio content could be delivered rapidly and in pristine quality to any place in the world with an Internet connection.

"Well, Fr. Roderick, I think we should do it!" he said as he stood up. "How long are you going to be in Rome? I would love it if you could talk to my colleagues and explain to them how to set up a podcast."

Wow! I never expected him to immediately embrace this idea. And now he wanted me to help the Vatican to set up a podcast? I was stunned.

"I guess I can reschedule my flight to a later date and stay a bit longer," I said.

"Brilliant! Let me introduce you to the tech-savvy people around here."

Later that same day, I found myself sitting at a computer with a couple of people, showing them the technical details of setting up a podcast feed. A few days later, Vatican Radio launched its first official podcast feed. As a result, the Vatican was one of the first big institutions in the world to use this technology.

White Smoke

Less than two weeks after the death of John Paul II, I was back in the Vatican. I had purchased a cheap airline ticket and was staying at the Dutch Pontifical College because I absolutely wanted to be in Rome during the conclave. This was history in the making, and I wanted to report on it. I secretly hoped that I would be in St. Peter's Square recording the moment when the new pope was announced. But I also felt this was an incredible opportunity to give the world an inside look at the Catholic Church when a huge worldwide audience was looking for information. My podcast had continued to grow, and almost ten thousand people were now downloading each new episode as soon as it was posted online.

The cardinals had all arrived in Rome for the general congregations, which is a series of meetings at the Vatican's Synod Hall before the start of a conclave. The cardinals discuss the rules of the conclave as well as a wide range of issues the Church is facing. During these pre-conclave meetings, certain cardinals can make their mark and get noticed by their colleagues as potential candidates for the papacy. As you can imagine, those meetings are closed to the press. And yet, I had already been able to show my listeners a glimpse of the events leading up to the conclave.

The day before the funeral of John Paul II, I heard that a special Mass would be celebrated at St. Peter's Basilica in honor of the late pope. The Mass wouldn't take place at the central altar, but at the altar underneath the chair of St. Peter and the oval stained-glass window that depicts the Holy Spirit in the form of a dove. As usual, priests were allowed to concelebrate. To go to the sacristy, I had to use the left entrance to the Vatican, past the two Swiss Guards that are always on watch. I knew that on my way to the Basilica, I would pass by the Synod Hall where the cardinals were gathering for their meetings. This was my chance. I decided to take my audio recorder with me and briefly record my impressions while walking past the building. I was a little nervous about this because I had no official accreditation as a journalist or a reporter. Were the Swiss Guards going to stop me and search me for equipment? I had my white alb folded over my left arm, and I held my digital recorder underneath it. My heart was beating fast, but to my relief, the guards saluted me and let me pass.

While I was walking, I bumped into several cardinals coming from the direction of the Synod Hall. I assumed that the morning session had just ended, and when I turned the corner, I could see at least forty cardinals standing outside in the sun, talking to each other. I couldn't believe my luck. Not many people were able to witness this, and certainly not the general press. And here I was, recording my impressions and looking at this group of cardinals that would elect the new pope!

On the right side of the square, I noticed a familiar cardinal.

"I see Cardinal Ratzinger over there," I told my virtual audience, the people who, in the future, would listen to this recording. "He is one of the most important people here at the Vatican. When the pope was ill, he was the one who led the Church and provided direction." As the dean of the College of Cardinals, he knew all his colleagues very well. He was greeting French Cardinal Lustiger, after which he effortlessly switched back from French to Italian.

"We could be looking at the next pope; he might be standing right beside us on this square," I said.

Late in the afternoon on April 19, digital recorder in hand, I joined the crowds in St. Peter's Square, not far from the central balcony above the entrance. It had taken me several hours to make my way through the hundreds of thousands of people staring at the small chimney on the roof of the Sistine Chapel. There had been two voting sessions in the morning, which both ended in black smoke. Would there be another voting session at the end of the day? No one knew for sure.

Suddenly, the crowd became agitated. Small puffs of smoke started to appear around the chimney. But at this time of the day, without direct sunlight, it was hard to make out the color of the smoke. Was it white? Was it gray? After fourteen agonizing minutes of confusion, I noticed that the big bells of the basilica started to move. While the sound of the bells echoed over the square, the crowd roared. We had a new pope! When the doors of the balcony above us finally opened, I pointed my microphone toward Cardinal Jorge Medina Estévez who appeared. *This is it!* I thought as I climbed on the gray plastic chair behind me to get a better view.

"Dear brothers and sisters," the cardinal said in various languages, after which he continued in Latin: *"Annuntio vobis gaudium magnum: Habemus Papam!"* The applause and cheers around me were deafening. *"Eminentissimum ac reverendissimum Dominum, Dominum Iosephum..."*

And that's when I knew. "Joseph Ratzinger!" I exclaimed into my microphone. "It's Ratzinger!"

Cardinal Medina confirmed my guess: *"Sanctæ Romanæ Ecclesiæ Cardinalem Ratzinger."*

When Pope Benedict XVI entered the balcony, I realized that I was witnessing another historic moment for the Catholic Church. And I was able to share it with thousands and thousands of listeners all around the world.

The Golden Ticket

So this is how Charlie Bucket must have felt, I thought, *when he stood in front of the imposing chocolate factory, about to meet Mr. Willy Wonka himself. Intimidated. Nervous. Overwhelmed. Excited.* For the twentieth time, I looked at the precious piece of paper that I held in my hand. My very own "golden ticket"! At least, that's what it looked like to me; in reality, it was yellow. It was decorated with a coat of arms, an official stamp with the number 28 on it, the date and, written in Italian: *"Incontro con il Santo Padre Benedetto XVI."* I was about to meet the pope in person! I swallowed and looked around me.

The Paul VI Hall was filled with approximately five thousand people. They were all active in Catholic media—from journalists and publishers to bloggers and parish volunteers from all over Italy. We had just had an audience with Pope Benedict XVI that concluded a conference on digital media and the Church. The pope had encouraged the participants to navigate the digital waters without fear with the same passion that has steered the ship of the Church for two thousand years. According to Benedict XVI, Catholics should inhabit this universe with hearts full of faith, thus giving the Internet a soul. I felt tremendously encouraged by these words. They mirrored the way I had tried to work in new media for a long time: being present in social networks, in the world of podcasts and online videos, not just with a message but with my heart and soul.

I totally expected to be seated somewhere in the middle of this big crowd, but right before I entered the hall, one of the conference organizers led me to a side entrance where I was able to sit in the front row, just a few steps away from Pope Benedict!

"The conference speakers will be allowed to meet the pope in person at the end," he said while handing me the yellow piece of paper with the invitation. I was so excited that I decided to use my phone to film a short video of the line forming in front of the pope, who was standing on a small, slightly elevated platform.

Benedict XVI is a relatively small man, and the platform allowed him to talk with his guests at eye level. I was still filming while advancing step-by-step when one of the guards that surrounded us pointed at my phone and shook his head. *"Padre, no video per favore."* Slightly flustered, I hastily put the phone back into my pocket and waited for my turn.

I happened to be the last in line. My mind was racing. *What should I say to the pope? Should I address him in German? Italian? English?* Before I could make a decision, it was my turn. I stepped forward and knelt while kissing the pope's fisherman's ring as a sign of respect. A cardinal next to the pope introduced me in Italian. "Holy Father, this is Fr. Roderick Vonhögen from the Netherlands; he also spoke at our conference." Pope Benedict grabbed both of my hands and looked at me intently. I noticed how soft his hands were. All my nervousness disappeared; I felt totally at ease. It was almost as if I were talking to my grandfather. I told him about my work in new media and podcasting and how grateful I was for his encouragement to continue to use new media to reach out to the world. Pope Benedict XVI listened attentively and then thanked me. It was an extraordinary moment in my life as a priest. This meeting was a tremendous affirmation of what I had been trying to do in new media for years! I couldn't have been more thankful.

CHAPTER FIVE

Health and Holiness

Coffee and Popcorn

"You look sleepy!" the Ethiopian driver told me while his white van slowly climbed up the mountain. It was still early in the morning, and outside my window, I could see the busy capital city of Addis Ababa beneath me.

"I didn't have time to drink a cup of coffee," I told him. "We have to start filming early today!"

"Oh, don't worry," he replied, "you will get coffee where we are going. The family will want to honor you with our traditional Ethiopian coffee ceremony!"

For the first time in my life, I was in Africa. Each year during Lent, the bishops of the Netherlands encourage people to support a specific charity. That year, they had chosen the work of the Daughters of Charity, religious sisters working among the poor in the city of Addis Ababa. I was asked to travel to Ethiopia to film a number of short television documentaries on location in order to give people an idea what was going on and why their help was needed.

I had no idea what to expect. You don't get to see much of Africa in our Western media. International news agencies don't have many reporters in African countries, and even if there is something serious going on, it hardly ever makes the front page of our newspapers. We often talk about Africa as if it were a single country where it's hot and where people are poor. In reality, it is a huge continent with an astonishing variety of peoples and cultures. This was a big eye-opener to me during my time in Rome, when I studied with priests from all over the world, and many of my fellow students in the social communications program were from Africa. They told me stories about life in Uganda, about the tension between Christians and Muslims in Nigeria, about the horrors of the civil war in Sierra Leone, about the importance of soccer in Ghana, and about the love of music in Kenya.

So, what did I know about Ethiopia? Not much. The country had one of the oldest Christian cultures of the continent; it produced fabulous marathon runners and, according to legend, it was the country where coffee was first discovered. The first thing I noticed after landing on the tarmac of the huge international airport of Addis Ababa was the thin air. I was already out of breath just carrying my luggage from the airport exit to the taxi parking lot. The city of roughly four million inhabitants is located at a relatively high altitude. Apparently, that is one of the reasons why Ethiopian long-distance runners are among the best in the world: Most of them are from high-altitude regions and have adapted to the smaller amount of oxygen in the air. This makes them much stronger than other runners at lower altitudes, where most races are held.

The city of Addis Ababa is a fascinating mix of old and new, poor and rich. In the distance, I could see skyscrapers being built in the commercial district, but we headed for the older part of the city. Most of the smaller roads were bumpy and full of gigantic holes. The main roads were overcrowded with incredibly old cars and blue-and-white taxis. Because of sky-high import taxes, there were very few new cars in the country. The taxis we took were often thirty to forty years old, and these rusty vehicles were patched up year after year with scrap metal and duct tape. Most people were too poor to own a car or even a bike, so typically everybody walked—women wrapped in colorful robes, carrying large bundles of whatever they were going to sell at the market; men dressed in white, on their way to one of the old Ethiopian orthodox churches; and small kids ran in sandals between the shoe shiners and the beggars sleeping on the side of the road.

But here, up on the mountain, everything was much calmer. I saw a group of women carrying stones near the construction site of a new church. We drove past a small marketplace with tiny shops on the side where people displayed their wares on the dusty ground of the square. When we reached the top of the hill, the family we would meet that morning was waiting for us outside their house. Admittedly, *house* was probably not the right word for it: It was nothing but a small cabin made out of mud and sheets of plastic. The mother proudly showed me their living room—a small square room with gray walls and a hole that functioned as a window. The walls were plastered with colorful holy pictures, and a tiny old television was playing in the corner. Our driver, who also served as our translator that day, told me that the family probably borrowed the television from another family just to make a good impression on us. Two young children sat on a small sofa while the older daughters stood in the doorway because there was no more room for them. One of them was pregnant; she couldn't have been more than fourteen years old.

The mother gestured that we should sit on the well-worn sofa that occupied half the room, and she began heating up a few coals in a small stove.

"I told you they would serve you coffee," the driver said. "This coffee ceremony is a very old tradition in Ethiopia. It is a sign of hospitality with which they want to honor your presence."

The ritual unfolded like a liturgy. After burning and grinding the coffee beans, the coffee was brewed in a small pot on the hot coals and then poured into small porcelain cups on a miniature table, which was decorated like a small altar. The smell of coffee filled the room. The mother handed me a cup, smiled, and said something I couldn't understand.

"She is asking if you want popcorn," the driver translated. She placed a big bowl of white popcorn on the table. "This is a great sacrifice for this family," the translator continued. "Normally, they only eat at the end of the day, but they saved up enough money to prepare this popcorn for you."

These people had almost nothing, and yet they shared all this with me. I felt embarrassed taking a handful of the white popcorn. I used to mindlessly eat a bucket of this stuff while watching a movie on Saturday evening, whereas here, popcorn was a precious gift worth a day's wages.

My habit of snacking on chips and junk food had caused me to be seriously overweight. Not obese, but firmly in the orange zone. Without my really noticing, the numbers on the scale had started to creep up more and more. In seminary, we were always served balanced meals, but the downside of that was that I hadn't learned much about nutrition or healthy eating. As a priest, I had to cook for myself and, due to a lack of time, I had developed the habit of eating TV dinners, pizza, or Chinese takeaway. And after a long day of stressful work, I often ate entire bags of potato chips, telling myself that I deserved it.

I had seen documentaries about famine in Africa, with the malnourished children and their desperate parents. And yet it never hit home—until now. For the price of one bag of chips, I could have fed an entire Ethiopian family for a day. And so, inspired by my experiences in Ethiopia, I decided to make some radical changes. It was time for some new routines.

From Couch Potato to Marathon Runner

I can't remember what triggered it, but on a Monday morning soon after I returned from Ethiopia, I decided I wanted to go out for a run. I was overweight, I wasn't fit, and I was sick and tired of being sick and tired. I wanted to change! In my closet, I found a pair of sneakers I had bought while on vacation, and on the top shelf, I discovered a dark blue tracksuit I had never used. I headed out the door and started running. After five minutes I had to stop because I thought I was going to die. I was gasping for breath, and I felt a sharp stitch in my side. I walked a bit to catch my breath and tried to run some more. It was useless. After a few more seconds, I had to stop again. My feet were hurting, my heart was racing, and I was sweating like crazy.

This was never going to work.

The next day, I ached all over. I felt muscles I didn't even know I had. And yet, I wanted to try again. To my surprise, I was able to run a bit more, and I didn't feel as exhausted as I did the first day. I told myself that the next time, I would try to make it all the way to a bridge over the canal I saw in the distance. And I did. I challenged myself to reach the next bridge without stopping, and lo and behold: On the fourth day, I was able to make it to that bridge as well!

I started to talk about my new running activity on my weekly podcast and immediately received enthusiastic feedback from a number of my listeners. It turned out that many of them were experienced runners. They gave me some great advice.

"You have to get yourself a pair of good shoes!" Steve wrote. "If you continue to run wearing those sneakers, you are going to injure yourself!"

"Try to find a running schedule," wrote Jeanne. "There are some really good training schedules online that will help you enhance your distances and improve your speed in a responsible manner. And keep telling us how it goes!"

And that's what I did. With the proper shoes and a good training schedule, I was making great progress. I started to lose weight. I felt a lot more energetic than ever before, and running outside also lifted my spirits. After a couple of weeks, I was hooked. I was no longer a couch potato. I was now a runner!

At the time, I was managing SQPN, the multimedia organization I founded with Greg and Jennifer Willits in 2005. Greg had also started to run. One day, he told me his crazy idea: "There is a marathon in Atlanta in October, and I want to participate," he said.

"You're out of your mind!" I told him. "Do you realize what you are talking about? I just Googled it: 26.2 miles through the streets of Atlanta; that's 42.195 kilometers! And Atlanta is not like Holland; there are some steep hills you'd have to climb!"

"I know," he said, "but I found a training schedule online that maps out the entire training process. If I start now, I can be ready for the race in October. I need a goal. I can't just go out for a run without a purpose. I want to reach for something!"

He had a point. Without a specific goal, it was way too easy to skip a training run. Excuses are easy to find when you don't feel like running: too much e-mail, rainy weather, a website that needs updating, or the living room that needs to be cleaned. Perhaps I also needed a goal to keep me motivated and on track.

"If you really want to run that marathon, I will run it with you!" I said. And so I started my marathon training.

Over the next couple of months, our listeners heard stories about our progress and setbacks. They also noticed that running began to influence my entire lifestyle, including my spiritual life. Running requires endurance and consistency. You can't give up too easily because skipping a training session causes you to fall behind schedule, so you might not be ready in time for the race. That same discipline started to bear fruit in other areas of my life. From planning my work to praying, I noticed that I was gradually developing much more discipline than I had ever had before. I had a long way to go, though. My scale told me I was still overweight, and even though I was burning a lot more calories than I used to, I still hadn't changed my habit of eating fatty food and salty snacks.

What gave me the final push toward eating healthier and developing a more balanced lifestyle? A television show called *The Biggest Loser*.

The Biggest Loser

The idea behind *The Biggest Loser* was simple: Bring together two teams of overweight people, give them a pair of trainers, and have them compete over several months to find the person who could lose the most weight. The program enjoyed a lot of success over the years because of the blend of entertainment, reality TV, and health information. Obesity is a growing problem in our Western countries, and many people struggle with their weight and self-image. Seeing men and women effectively turn their lives around made for uplifting, motivating television. What struck me most was that obesity and food addiction are hardly ever the result of laziness or stupidity. Over the course of each season, the trainers would uncover personal traumas or unresolved conflicts that led to self-medicating with food. It was almost never enough to combat the symptoms by putting the contestants on a diet and forcing them to spend hours at the gym each day; in order to obtain lasting change, the underlying problems needed to be dealt with.

That TV show made me think. *Why did I develop these unhealthy eating habits? Did I have any problems I was subconsciously struggling with that had led to my behavior?* I had never given it much thought before I started to watch *The Biggest Loser*, but these questions started to occupy my mind more and more. At the same time, I had noticed how much my new running passion had started to positively affect my spiritual life and my working discipline. What if I were to record a podcast about these topics—something about the connection between body, mind, and soul, about how to get physically healthy, but also about how to maintain a healthy spiritual life? The series *Health and Holiness* was born.

Every one or two weeks, I would record a podcast after completing a run or while going for a walk outside. While walking, I would simply talk about the things that occupied my mind that day. The show had two overarching goals: a reflection on how to live a healthy and balanced life, and a question that was perhaps even more important: how to live a holy life.

It was during those walks that I began to discover a few of the issues hampering my progress toward a more balanced life. They were old issues, really. One of them was stress. The old people pleaser in me was still alive and well, and there were times that I said yes to way too many things. At the same time, I would feel guilty for not being able to handle the huge piles of e-mail sitting in my inbox. What would people think of me if I didn't respond to them? I spent too much time every day trying to process e-mails and dealing with all sorts of promises I had made. Then, if I got too overwhelmed and my stress levels got too high, I would overeat.

Another problem was my fear of being judged by others. Somewhere deep down, I could still sense the presence of that nerdy boy who got teased and pushed around by the local school bullies. The social networks I was engaging in had their share of bullies, too. After each interview on television, these bullies would appear in my Twitter timeline, making nasty comments. For some, I was an ultraconservative idiot, while others thought I was an attention-crazy liberal priest who embodied everything that was wrong with the priesthood. No matter how much my mind told me that these comments said more about the people who uttered them than about me, the criticism still managed to get under my skin way too often. No matter how many positive e-mails I received, one nasty, accusatory message could totally derail me and depress me for days.

However, I discovered that I wasn't the only one struggling with these issues. Because I was sharing them with a large audience, many people wrote that they could identify with the things I was talking about. Instead of pretending to be someone who knew it all and was never fazed by anything or anyone, I discovered that by talking about my vulnerabilities, I was helping others come to terms with their own weak spots.

Balanced Living

I had known Cliff Ravenscraft for several years. He had started podcasting around the same time as I did, and he had successfully developed a business based on teaching others how to podcast. One of my favorite podcasts was one he produced together with Stephanie, his wife—a fan podcast about the television series *Lost*. His approach to podcasting was very similar to mine: Take a popular franchise, gather a community of listeners, and produce a lively, personal show with good information and, at times, deeper discussions about the broader themes of the story.

Cliff's ability to build a strong, personal bond with his listeners was impressive. The community around his *Lost* podcast wasn't like any other fan community: It offered a warm and friendly environment for people who missed such an environment where they lived. There was Anne-Sophie, a young woman from Germany, who had battled anorexia for many years. When she was at her lowest point, she discovered the television show *Lost* and the community around Cliff and Stephanie's podcast. She later told me it saved her life. Thanks to the friendship and encouragement of her new online friends, she was able to overcome her situation and slowly rebuild her life. She is now a podcaster herself, encouraging others with eating disorders not to give up.

Cliff, too, was a great fan of *The Biggest Loser* TV show. He was trying to change his habits and pursue a more balanced, healthful life, just like me. Why not record a podcast series about this show together? And that's what we did. Our podcast was more than just a weekly discussion about what happened to the contestants on TV. We were trying to put everything we learned into practice, sharing it via social networks with our followers, and I have rarely felt so motivated. At first, it was quite daunting to confess our failures if we had caved and overeaten during the week. But soon, our listeners started to send us voicemails sharing their own failures, setbacks, and successes. Both the podcast and the social networks we used became a way to create accountability. Nothing proved more helpful than the thought that other people were doing their best to reach the same ideals and goals as we were.

Meanwhile, I was still training for a marathon. My first attempt to get ready for the Atlanta Marathon had failed. I made the classic mistake of ignoring the training schedule, and I injured myself by running too much and too often. Greg Willits did run the marathon, however, and I traveled to Georgia to film his run and share in the experience. Now, a year later, I was training for a marathon that was being organized in my own city of Amersfoort to celebrate its 750th anniversary.

I used a whole slew of gadgets to enhance my running experience. For example, I had special running shoes with an electronic sensor in them that wirelessly connected to my iPhone. The sensor counted my steps and kept track of my distance and pace. Later, I used a GPS-based running app that could generate a map of the route I had run and post it automatically on Facebook and Twitter. There were even apps that would post a message on Facebook at the start of a run, and whenever someone posted an encouraging comment, the app would receive a signal over the

Internet and play the sound of people cheering. It sounds goofy, but things like this can be a huge motivation during a long, lonely run in the countryside.

The most creative app I have ever used for my training runs contained zombies. At the start of each run, I would listen to an episode of a radio play about a post-apocalyptic world in which I was on the run from zombies. I had to run between outposts of refugees, finding food and medicine along the way. And every once in a while, I would stumble upon a group of zombies, and the app calculated via GPS if I was running fast enough to escape them!

Fortunately, on the day of my first marathon, there were no zombies in sight. My parishioners were cheering on the side of the road, and I thoroughly enjoyed the experience. Things only got tough when my iPhone's battery died and I didn't know how much farther I had to run. I thought I was almost done, but my heart sank when I discovered that I still had much more of the course left than I expected. However, I did make it to the finish line, and my first thought was, *I want to run another one!*

I still enjoy running on a regular basis. It allows me to listen to podcasts, reflect on my life, pray, and come up with new ideas. And even though Cliff and I eventually ended our podcast about *The Biggest Loser*, we still talk regularly about our endeavors in new media, community building, and balanced living. It is amazing how much both of our communities have turned into places where people feel at home and encourage each other in friendship.

Runner's Tips for Wannabe Saints

My podcast series is called *Health and Holiness*. There are lots of practical ways to increase your health: eating a balanced diet, running, exercising, avoiding stress, sleeping enough, living an organized life. But what about holiness? Isn't that just for saints, those extraordinary people who lived heroic lives and acquired impressive spiritual insights? However, when Jesus told his disciples to "be perfect, just as your heavenly Father is perfect," he wasn't just addressing a small group of superheroes. Holiness is a calling we all receive on the day of our baptism.

But *how* do you become a saint?

"First of all, you will have to die," Fr. Marc said, grinning, when I asked him the question. As a Jesuit, he was working at the Generalate of his order in Rome and was tasked with preparing the beatification and canonization of his fellow Jesuits. I was interviewing him about his vocation and his work, and I figured he would be the perfect person to tell me how to become a saint.

"Is there anything I should do before dying in order to become a saint?" I asked.

"Do you have a Facebook page and a Twitter account?" Fr. Marc asked me with a twinkle in his eye.

"Of course!"

"Delete them! And while you're at it, also delete all your blogs, empty your e-mail archives, and destroy all your letters and diaries."

I was more than a little taken aback by this advice. "Why would I do that?"

"Because the more you write, the more there is to examine, and the less likely it is that you will make it through the entire canonization process. Every nook and cranny of your life on earth will be examined. After all, when the Church declares someone to be a saint, it wants to be sure that you really were one! Really, the less you write, the easier it will be for us to get you through the process."

I didn't dare tell him about the thousands of podcasts and blog posts I have generated over the years. I knew that Fr. Marc was half joking, but what he said was true. For most of us, tons of things we did and wrote can be found all over the Internet. The silly photos of our vacation are on Facebook, that video in which you teased your dog by dressing him up as Darth Vader is posted on YouTube, and the angry comments you posted on Twitter or in the comments section of your blog might be circulating in cyberspace long after you are gone.

Unless I followed the advice of this Dutch Jesuit priest to eradicate my entire online presence, I knew it was highly unlikely that I would ever be canonized. One advantage: There was no need to reserve my bones or cassock for the production of relics. However, the unlikeliness of ever being canonized didn't mean that I wasn't called to holiness. Quite the contrary! After all, a canonization is only the public recognition of a holy life. There are many more holy men and women than will ever be officially canonized.

Perhaps holiness is a bit like running. You train, you sacrifice time and effort, you run a race, but you never get to be first—but you still keep running. Why? Because it's not about the medal; it's about running and living a healthy life!

Here are my runner's tips for wannabe saints:

Running a marathon begins with running the first mile. If you don't get off the couch, you'll never get anywhere. In the same way, holiness begins with the resolution to become holy. You have to take the first step. Start reserving time in your life to live with God. Make it a firm appointment in your agenda if you are busy.

You'll never finish if you don't set a goal. I would never have run a marathon if I hadn't made it a goal to do so. Setting a goal has an incredibly motivating effect. It represents something to strive for, something that will motivate you even when you don't feel like training. The same is true for your spiritual life. You need to set spiritual goals—the more specific and concrete, the better.

Progress is made by training and constantly pushing your boundaries. Every running schedule slowly increases the distances. Praying requires similar persistence. It is something you learn over time. At first, it can be very difficult to be still for more than a minute. Don't give up. Keep trying to reserve a bit more time every day. You will see that, after a while, it gets easier.

Be sure you have the right equipment. You need to equip yourself with the right gear: a good pair of shoes; light, breathable clothing in the summer and layered clothes in the winter; a water bottle; a hat to protect you from the sun; and perhaps a GPS device to track your runs. For your spiritual life, you also need the right equipment. You will definitely need a Bible, other spiritual books, and a place in your home dedicated to prayer, perhaps with images, candles, and other things that help you focus on God.

Follow a training schedule. To prepare for a 5K, a half-marathon, or a marathon, it's important to follow a training schedule. I used the schedules created by Hal Higdon that contained daily advice on how far to run, when to rest, and when to push yourself. The Church proposes schedules and routines that can help you make progress in your spiritual life, too. The Liturgy of the Hours takes you by the hand and suggests prayers and readings for every moment of the day. The Sunday obligation is another important tool: Just as you need a regular routine to make any progress in sports, creating a habit of going to Mass on Sunday (and even on weekdays if you can) will be a great help to grow in faith. The Church even offers special times of training, like Lent or Advent. The more you invest in your spiritual training, the more it will transform you.

Seek advice from other runners. While I was training for my first marathon, I loved listening to podcasts from other runners. Their experience helped me a lot. Some of my parishioners were also experienced runners, and they helped me avoid common mistakes while training. Your spiritual progress can also benefit from good advice. Find a spiritual director, and share your journey with friends, either in your local community or perhaps even via the Internet. Sharing your spiritual struggles and progress can help others, and it will benefit you, too. And don't forget the saints! They have shown that it is possible to live a holy life. Read about their lives and take advantage of their experience!

Don't overdo it. One of the biggest pitfalls for beginning runners is running too much. I made that mistake in my first year of running. I felt I could go faster and farther than the training schedule prescribed. The result? An injury that prevented me from running for several months! There was also a drop in my motivation as a consequence. I learned to pace myself and to train in moderation.

Your spiritual life requires a similar balance. Develop reasonable habits. Don't expect to pray for hours every day, or to be constantly, 100 percent focused on God and ready to receive the most beautiful mystical experiences. You might disappoint yourself if you can't keep it up. Take small steps first, and let the Holy Spirit guide the process.

Don't give up too quickly. All runners have moments when they want to give up. Long training runs in the cold can be trying. You start to think about the warm couch in your living room, a good book, a cup of hot chocolate. You start to wonder why on earth are you running outside when you would have been so much more comfortable had you stayed home. A temporary injury that interrupts your training might make you discouraged and ready to give up because you might not be ready in time for the marathon. Well, it might be better to run a half-marathon instead of completely giving up.

In your spiritual life, there will be many times you might be tempted to give up. Sometimes praying is easy, but often it can be difficult and require willpower. Just like love, prayer depends more on an act of the will than on a feeling. If you only pray or go to Church when you feel like it, you won't make much progress. There are going to be tough days, moments—sometimes even months or years—when you feel like you are traveling through a spiritual desert. Don't beat yourself up about it. Don't give up. Take small steps, and trust God to accompany you. Keep moving forward despite temporary setbacks. These are normal; it's how God tests your resolve.

Stay hydrated and pay attention to what you eat. This is vitally important for any long-distance runner. Your muscles need energy, and energy comes from food. That is why runners often eat lots of pasta before a big run: It helps the body store enough energy to complete the run. Dehydration can be very dangerous, especially when the weather is warm. So always take water with you, or make sure water is provided during your races.

In your spiritual life, good nutrition and hydration are just as important. Here I'm not just referring to the prayer books you take with you to the chapel. We are constantly consuming information and entertainment, but just like junk food can have nefarious consequences for our health, so can junk media. Without becoming overly scrupulous, ask yourself whether or not a book, a movie, a video game, or other forms of entertainment are really enriching your life. Good content can enrich your spiritual life; trash media can hamper it. Be picky—it's for your own good!

Enjoy the process! The most important advice I ever got from a runner right before my first marathon was to enjoy it! Don't worry about speed, winning, or performance. Run at your own pace, look around you, and take it all in. Enjoy the run itself; it will give you energy. I found all this to be very true. I crossed the finish line with a big grin on my face. I hadn't run particularly fast, but I had fun! I felt so thankful to have been able to complete the race.

This also applies to your spiritual life. Don't approach it as a burden or a duty! Don't beat yourself up about not doing enough. Look at prayer as a joyful moment with God. He is looking forward to spending some time with you, and you should look forward to it, too! If you have trouble praying, or if you feel lazy and uninspired, don't force your way through your prayer time. Instead, just start thanking God for all the graces, big and small, in your life. Name every positive experience you've had over the past few days and thank God for each of them. You will notice that it will cheer you up and bring joy back to your prayer times. Thanksgiving is one of the most powerful forms of prayer.

CHAPTER SIX

Hobbits, Angels, and Wizards

Saints and Soap Operas

After the events in the Vatican, life returned to normal. I was back in the Netherlands, working in my parishes and thinking about the next step. How could I continue to use new media to reach out? There was a huge interest about what happened in Rome after the death of John Paul II and the election of Pope Benedict XVI, but how could I keep the momentum going without all this excitement? After all, you don't get a new pope every month!

Could I come up with other topics that might be of interest to my current audience? Would it be possible to reach even more people, especially those who were not Catholic or who had lost contact with the Church? During my studies in social communications at the Gregorian University, I had learned that communication and community building always takes place around shared content. In order to feel part of a community, you need to have something in common.

This was one of the great discoveries of the 1940s and 1950s, leading to the invention of the soap opera. The soap industry wanted to target an audience of homemakers with their advertising. But how could they reach that demographic? They came up with daytime radio plays and later television series aimed at women, aired every day with continuing storylines designed to keep the audience watching to see what would happen next.

During these shows, the soap companies would feature commercials showcasing their products. Over the years, the format became hugely popular. Since there weren't as many channels on TV then as there are now, everybody was watching the same shows, and everybody was talking about them, thereby increasing and solidifying the audience for these series.

Today, the number of television, radio, and Internet channels is almost infinite. And yet, even today there are movies, television series, books, or games that appeal to a global audience. I've already mentioned *Star Wars*, but there is a similar worldwide interest for J.K. Rowling's *Harry Potter* books, superhero movies like *Iron Man* or the *Avengers*, *Star Trek*, *Lost*, Disney movies, *The Hobbit,* and *The Lord of the Rings*. Even certain brands have gathered a worldwide fan base: Apple, Microsoft, Nintendo, Google. And what do all these different fan communities do? They talk about their common interests! They share their enthusiasm for upcoming movies or products and speculate about what's coming next.

There had to be a way to tap into those communities. Fortunately, I have very eclectic interests, ranging from technology to theology, from cooking to running, from movies to video games. So I created a show that combined all those interests into one program, which I called *The Daily Breakfast*. Later, when I switched to a weekly schedule, I renamed it *The Break*. I formatted it to be a lighthearted, morning-show type of program, but I included a segment in which I answered listeners' questions about the Catholic faith.

In the meantime, I had discovered other Catholics who, just like me, had started to record podcasts. It is interesting to note that most of these Catholic podcasters were laypeople. Greg and Jennifer Willits recorded a weekly show about the way they tried to live their faith and run their twine-knotted rosary apostolate; Mac and Katherine Barron formed another podcasting couple who talked about movies, books, and family happenings with a great sense of humor. Paul Camerata was a neurosurgeon with a passion for saints who used his podcast, *SaintCast,* to talk about the lives of saints and martyrs. Lisa Hendey was a Catholic mom who blogged and podcasted about, well, being a Catholic mom. A Franciscan priest who taught Church history at the Franciscan University of Steubenville was the author of a show called *Catholic Under the Hood* in which he told riveting stories about key moments in Catholic history. David and Allyson Sweeney from Texas even involved their children in their episodes of *The Catholic Family.* These and many other podcasters were at the forefront of a revolution in Catholic media. No longer was audio-visual media production restricted to large companies or institutions—anyone with a microphone and an Internet connection could reach out to a worldwide audience.

The Magi

In 2005, Pope Benedict XVI traveled to the German city of Cologne for World Youth Day. It was his first foreign trip as the new pope, and more than a million young Catholics were expected to attend. I was excited. Cologne was just a few hours away from where I lived in the Netherlands. I could easily do the same thing I had done during the conclave in Rome: bring my digital audio recorder and take my listeners with me to experience the event from the inside.

On the eve of World Youth Day, I was walking among the hundreds of thousands of young people, priests, deacons, and nuns who had spread out their sleeping bags at the foot of an enormous podium built on a hill. We were going to camp outdoors for the entire night and celebrate Mass with the pope the following morning. The atmosphere was incredible. The universal Church couldn't be more visible than that evening. Everywhere I walked, I heard chatter, songs, and music from all over the world, and everyone was friendly and relaxed. After all, we had gathered for the same thing.

That evening the pope talked about this same sense of community in a beautiful meditation on the story of the wise men from the East. Since the Middle Ages, pilgrims have traveled to Cologne to venerate the remains of the Magi at the cathedral, and our gathering that evening was like a big, global pilgrimage.

"Here in Cologne we discover the joy of belonging to a family as vast as the world," Pope Benedict said, "including heaven and earth, the past, the present, the future, and every part of the earth. In this great band of pilgrims, we walk side-by-side with Christ; we walk with the star that enlightens our history." Meeting the newborn King changed the Magi for good, symbolized by the new itinerary they would take on their way back home: "They will no longer ask: How can this serve me? Instead, they will have to ask: How can I serve God's presence in the world?"

These words somehow struck a chord with me. This was literally what I was doing at that moment. Thanks to the medium of podcasting, I was walking side-by-side with a huge future audience of listeners, following the same star, searching for answers, trying to find God in our lives. Wasn't that the greatest thing the new media allowed us to do: to be travel companions of those trying to find direction in their lives?

When I got back from Germany, I talked at length with Greg and Jennifer Willits about all the things we could do with new media. The possibilities were endless. We didn't need a studio, technicians, or lots of equipment to make a podcast or a video. New media was cheap, fast, and flexible, and it would allow us to make very personal and creative programs that, thanks to the Internet, we could distribute to anyone on the planet. We were witnessing a media revolution in the making. What if we joined forces and formed a network of all these talented individuals? Together, we might be able to help each other reach an even higher level of quality. And so, in the fall of 2005, we founded a nonprofit organization to do just that. When I had to come up with a name, I thought of Pope Benedict's address in Cologne about the Magi. With our new media initiatives, we wanted to help people in their quest for the star, so we chose SQPN, the Star Quest Production Network, for our name.

We tried to model our approach to new media on the way God himself communicated in the story of the Magi. Just like the wise men from the East, many people are surrounded by a popular culture that is very different from the culture of the Church. In order to reach them, something needs to attract their attention and make them curious. The star of Bethlehem did just that. Our new media productions should try to do the same: find people where they are and appear on their horizon. Most people search the Internet to find information about topics they are interested in. What if our programs somehow showed up in the list of search results? Then again, if our target audience wasn't necessarily religious, chances were low that people would find our programs, simply because they wouldn't be using religious search terms. There is a wealth of great Catholic content on the Internet, but most of it is aimed at those who have already found the Child of Bethlehem. If we wanted to reach new audiences, we needed to offer a different type of program.

I started to experiment with new programs that, at first sight, seemed to have nothing to do with faith or religion. For example, I created shows about *The Lord of the Rings, Harry Potter, Battlestar Galactica, Narnia,* and the TV series *Babylon 5.* Just like *Star Wars,* superhero movies, and fairy tales, these big franchises all heavily borrowed from mythology and religious traditions. This would enable us to talk about faith as well because the themes in these stories were bigger and more universal than the imaginary world in which they took place. All we needed to do was to find Catholics who were just as passionate about these stories as they were passionate about their faith and convince them to help us create new programs.

This approach proved to be very effective. Soon, we had audiences of tens of thousands of people downloading our shows and talking about them online. Since we never tried to force religious themes and topics upon our listeners, but just mentioned them when it helped to better understand the stories we were discussing, we managed to reach a wide variety of people, many of whom weren't Catholic or even religious. But they felt respected in their own personal journey. I sometimes said it explicitly: "I am a Catholic priest, but you don't have to be a Catholic to enjoy these programs." To me, that was a vital element of the story of the Magi: God didn't force them to leave their home. There was no thunderous voice from the clouds commanding the wise men to convert. It was their own initiative, their own journey. God just provided guidance along the way.

Similarly, I felt that our network should provide a form of guidance for those listeners who wanted to go one step further. In addition to the low-threshold shows that talked about popular culture, I wanted to have a number of shows that would help build a community—shows hosted by travel companions the listeners could identify with. And wouldn't it be great if we could somehow offer people a live experience where they could watch the hosts recording the show and interacting with the rest of the community?

A friend of mine from the Netherlands, Mike Versteeg, had created a software program called "Vidblaster." With this software, I could broadcast my shows with multiple cameras via a live video stream so that listeners could join the recording as a live audience. This proved to be a lot of fun. Over time, the people in the audience started to know each other very well and began to form friendships. The most beautiful example was the love that blossomed between two listeners, Mike, who lived in Michigan and Denyse, who lived in New Brunswick, Canada. They met each other in our community, and today, they are happily married as a result!

The ultimate goal of our journey is Jesus himself. Once the Magi found him in Bethlehem, they offered him their gifts and received his love in exchange. Once people found our network and became part of the community, we wanted to offer them specific content that would help them deepen their relationship with Christ, learn about their faith, and support their prayer life.

Shows like the *SaintCast*, *iPadre*, *Catholic Laboratory*, *Catholic Under the Hood*, *Catholic Vitamins*, and many more formed the third layer of programs we offered. We even created a podcast called *Praystation Portable*, which enabled people to download the prayers of the Liturgy of the Hours onto a mobile device so they could pray on the road. We also provided daily Mass readings via the *Verbum Domini* podcast.

Little by little, we gained a huge audience that slowly transformed into a community of friends gathered around the common experience of listening to the same podcasts. Unlike traditional media, this felt more like a family instead of an organization or institution. We organized yearly conferences that brought together even more new media enthusiasts. And every once in a while, people would share with us the spiritual journey that our programs and the community had allowed them to make.

One family wrote to tell me how they listened to one of my podcasts about *Harry Potter* in their car while driving the kids to school, and they eventually discovered other shows on the network as well. Gradually, they became more and more fascinated by the Catholic topics we discussed on our programs, and ultimately, the whole family decided to get baptized at their local Catholic church.

Other people wrote about how listening to our podcasts and connecting to the rest of the community helped them think about their vocation in life. Some of them entered the seminary or religious orders. It was very humbling to receive testimonies like that. Somehow, God was using new media to touch the lives of many people who otherwise might have never discovered him. To be able to witness the fruits of our work was incredibly gratifying, and it motivated us to do even more!

Wizards and Muggles

I had never been to the movies with companions like these. On my left, wearing a white habit, was Fr. Juan Mighel, a priest from Puerto Rico; on my right were three other priests all dressed in black: Fr. Sean from Ireland, Fr. William from Scotland, and Fr. Marc, a colleague of mine from the Netherlands. Behind us and in front of us, the red seats of this old movie theater in the center of Rome were filled with families and kids.

"Are you sure this movie is going to be in English?" I asked Fr. Juan Mighel. Italians prefer dubbing their movies instead of using subtitles, but I couldn't get used to watching well-known English and American actors rattling off their lines in high-speed Italian.

"Absolutely—I have already seen it twice before in this theater!"

"Twice already? But the movie is brand new!"

"Yes, but I went to see it on the day of the premiere and also yesterday. I am a big fan!"

He clearly wasn't the only big fan in the theater. Most of the kids around us were chattering excitedly about the movie we were about to see.

"Mum, is there going to be another movie after *la Pietra Filosofale*? Will they also film *la Camera dei Segreti*?"

"I don't know, darling. I guess we will have to wait and see."

The boy wore a red and yellow scarf and a pair of round glasses; he switched between Italian and English with ease. His parents were probably expats living in Rome. His sister pointed a plastic wand at her brother.

"*Petrificus totalus!*" she giggled.

"Hush now, Chiara! The movie is about to begin," her mother said.

The lights went out and the first notes of an enchanting melody filled the theater. The movie opened with a little boy fast asleep in a small basket. There was a scar on his forehead in the shape of a lightning bolt. His name? Harry Potter.

Because I had spent every bit of spare time I had working on audio and video homework assignments for my studies, I had missed a lot of the initial excitement about the books by J.K. Rowling. The first books of the saga had been a tremendous success, motivating a whole new generation of kids to start reading again. But I knew nothing about *Harry Potter* when we were waiting in line to get our tickets.

Fr. Juan Mighel had been going on and on about the books.

"Not only is it a wonderful story, but it is laden with Christian symbolism."

"Really?" I asked. I had to admit that I was a bit skeptical. How could a story about wizardry contain Christian themes?

"Oh, you'll see. Keep an eye on what happens in the Forbidden Forest!"

"No spoilers!" I warned him. "I haven't read the books yet!"

Because I had been forewarned, I watched the movie with extra attention. The priest next to me had been right: Despite the fact that the story took place in an imaginary world with witches and wizards living alongside Muggles (normal people who knew nothing about magic or wizardry), I noticed a lot of themes and ideas that were clearly inspired by the Christian tradition.

At the beginning of the movie, a young orphan boy is entrusted to the care of his aunt and uncle who live with their own son on Privet Drive. Just like Moses, the boy is raised, unaware of his true lineage. He was told that his parents were layabouts who were

HOBBITS, ANGELS, AND WIZARDS

killed in a car accident. But on his eleventh birthday, he receives the invitation to become a student at the Hogwarts School of Witchcraft and Wizardry. That's where he learns the truth about his parents: They were killed while trying to protect him from the evil wizard Voldemort. For some reason, Voldemort hadn't been able to kill the boy, and his evil curse merely left a scar in the shape of a lightning bolt on Harry's forehead.

Harry is presented as a savior archetype. An ancient prophecy seemed to indicate that he was the Chosen One who would defeat Voldemort with a power this Dark Lord didn't possess. The name *Voldemort* is telling: This dark nemesis is afraid of death. *Vol de Mort* in French identifies him as "one who tries to escape death." Harry first encounters him in a dark forest, where Voldemort appears as a ghost-like figure, drinking the blood that streams from the side of a white unicorn he has just killed. We learn that the blood of this highly venerated, noble animal was the only thing that kept Voldemort alive.

At this point, Fr. Juan Mighel leaned toward me.

"You see? The unicorn! A well-known medieval symbol for Christ. And Voldemort drinks the blood from its side. It's crystal-clear Eucharistic symbolism."

He was right. This wasn't a coincidence. In Christian iconography, we often see Christ on the cross, with an angel gathering in a cup the blood and the water that streams from his side where the soldier's lance pierced it. "Whoever eats my flesh and drinks my blood has eternal life," Jesus said. Catholics believe that in every Mass, bread and wine is transformed in the Body and Blood of Christ through the power of the Holy Spirit. Voldemort commits a sacrilege by killing the unicorn and consuming its blood for selfish motives.

This was getting interesting. The story depicted Voldemort as an almost satanic character who tried to gain power and flee death by taking the lives of innocent people. Later in the story, he was accompanied by a huge snake. And just like the snake in the story of Adam and Eve, Voldemort tried to lure Harry into believing that life is all about power and domination instead of love and compassion. Harry slowly discovers that he is called to defeat his evil nemesis by using a force that is far more powerful than any magic. It is the same force that led his parents to sacrifice themselves to save their child when Voldemort tried to kill him: the power of love and friendship. The end of the saga mirrors the Gospel when, in their final confrontation, Harry Potter saves the wizarding world by his willingness to sacrifice his life for his friends. While a superficial appraisal of the story might lead people to believe that this is a dark story about occult powers and wizardry, a closer examination reveals that at its core, the *Harry Potter* saga is heavily inspired by Christian themes and motives. J.K. Rowling later said that she didn't want to make it too obvious that the main storyline of the saga was based on the Gospel; otherwise, she thought, people might be able to guess what would happen to Harry toward the end of the story.

All of this gave me an idea. What if I started a podcast about the hidden dimensions of the story? Surely there would be *Harry Potter* fans that would want to listen to such a show. With all the Christian themes woven into the story, this could be great material to educate a young audience about the Christian faith via stories with which they were very familiar. With millions of *Harry Potter* books already sold and more movies on the way, there was potentially a very large audience for such a show.

I was right. I gathered a small group of Catholic podcasters to join me in a weekly discussion about the books and the movies. After only a few episodes of the *Secrets of Harry Potter*, more than forty thousand *Harry Potter* fans were listening to our new show. Most of them had probably never been in contact with a priest before. I started to receive enthusiastic e-mails from all over the world. Parents loved that they could talk about faith with their kids using *Harry Potter*, thanks to the key I had provided them to unlock the deeper layers of the story.

Not everyone shared our enthusiasm for the *Harry Potter* story, though. We received some concerned e-mails from people who were convinced that the books were promoting occultism and superstition. Those concerns were understandable, especially if you hadn't read the books themselves. The Church has always condemned occultism and witchcraft. The problem is that these things lure people into believing that they can manipulate and dominate other people, and even the future, whereas faith is all about trusting God for guidance. "Whoever wishes to save his life will lose it, but whoever loses his life for my sake will find it," says Jesus.

However, having now read the entire *Harry Potter* series, I am of the opinion that this was exactly what the story wanted to illustrate. Voldemort was the terrifying personification of someone who, like Satan, completely rejected love and mercy, who used magic as a tool to subject people and events to his will. On the other hand, Harry learned that the greatest power in life is love, and that love leads to self-sacrifice. The selfless act of giving one's life away will ultimately lead to finding it.

My objective was to connect with the millions of *Harry Potter* fans around the world and discuss these deeper layers of the story in order to demonstrate how much the journey of Harry Potter was inspired by the journey of Jesus in the Gospels—pointing the way from an imaginary savior to the real one. To my delight, many of our listeners did discover that other Savior whose sacrifice inspired that of J.K. Rowling's hero. Angie, one of our listeners, let me know that she had found SQPN thanks to our *Harry Potter* show and had entered RCIA with her husband as a result of it. She is one of many, many people who have written me over the years about how our *Harry Potter* podcasts led them to rediscover the Catholic faith.

Harry Potter wasn't the only modern story that enabled us to build a bridge between popular culture and the Catholic faith. Another great saga was attracting huge audiences to the movies, and this saga was based on the writings of a devout Catholic author: J.R.R. Tolkien.

Podcasting in Middle-earth

It was a beautiful day in the Shire, and I was following the path up the hill that leads to Bag End, the underground home of Hobbit Bilbo Baggins. Birds were chirping, and a flock of sheep was grazing in the distance. To my left, in the valley below, I could see a small pond and next to it the enormous Party Tree under which Bilbo had performed his last disappearing act before traveling to Rivendell. At the entrance to Bilbo's home, I turned around to the person following me.

"James, I keep pinching myself to convince myself that I am not dreaming. I can't believe I am here!"

James grinned. "We Kiwis really know how to make an impression on foreigners, don't we?"

"I wish I didn't have to go back to the Netherlands. I wouldn't mind living in one of these Hobbit holes for the rest of my life. It is so beautiful and peaceful here!"

James Bergin was a Catholic podcaster living in Auckland, New Zealand's capital city. He was a longtime listener to the SQPN podcasts, and together with Gavin Abraham and a couple of other young Catholics, he had invited me to visit their beautiful country. Before that, I had spent about a week in Sydney, Australia, at the invitation of ACPA, the Australasian Catholic Press Association. During their annual convention, I had shared my experiences and adventures in the world of Catholic new media. It was a wonderful event. I had never traveled this far before, and the journalists and Catholic diocesan communication experts had been just as friendly and welcoming as the springtime weather on this side of the planet.

I was impressed by the incredible vitality of the Catholic Church in Australia. I visited the communications department of the neighboring diocese of Parramatta as well as the impressive press department of the Archdiocese of Sydney with their amazing Internet initiative, XT3.com. Cardinal Pell had told me how much the pope's visit in 2008 for World Youth Day had helped mobilize an entire new generation of young Catholics. One of them, the always-enthusiastic Jessica Langrell, had invited me to speak at their local Theology on Tap meeting. I expected a small group of ten to twenty participants, but instead I was stunned to see that hundreds of students and young adults had showed up to listen to my story.

There was another geeky reason that I was excited to be in Sydney. This was the city where the movie *The Matrix* had been filmed. Being a big fan of that surreal science-fiction movie, I had downloaded and printed a list of all the locations that are recognizable in the movie. One afternoon, I walked around for hours, trying to check them all off my list. The ACPA convention ended with a dinner, where I met Julie Goodwin. She had just won Australia's first season of *MasterChef*, a cooking program that had taken the country by storm. She was also a Catholic who volunteered in her local parish. In a wonderful talk, she shared her experience of being part of such a high-profile reality show. Her family and her friends at the parish had been a huge support, especially when the show was over and she discovered that she had turned into a national celebrity. Her parish priest was also sitting at our table, and he revealed himself to be a huge fan of *The Hobbit* and *The Lord of the Rings*. When he heard that I was planning to visit New Zealand the following week, he insisted that I try to visit Matamata, the place where Peter Jackson filmed the scenes in the Shire for *The Lord of the Rings*.

"You are aware that they are going back there to film *The Hobbit*, right?" he asked.

"Yes, but I don't know if it will be possible to visit the site. After all, I am only staying in New Zealand for a couple of days."

"Well, if you have the occasion, please give my regards to Fili, Kili, Oin, Gloin, Thorin, Dwalin, Balin, Bifur, Bofur, Bombur, Dori, Nori, and Ori. And Bilbo, of course."

Wow—this was the first priest I had ever met who could name the dwarfs in *The Hobbit* just as easily as the apostles of the Gospel!

"I will!" I promised. But would I find the time to get there? I highly doubted it.

Gavin, James, and my other hosts had kept the activities planned during my visit a surprise. After doing another talk about new media in Auckland, I had been a guest on their monthly Catholic talk show, *The Fifteenth Station*. I had listened to that podcast for a long time, and it was surreal to be part of the show and see the faces that belonged to the voices that had become so familiar over time. What also surprised me was how similar the culture in New Zealand is to the culture in Europe. It shouldn't be surprising, of course, since a large part of the current population originally came from my part of the world. And yet, small details told me that I was in a totally different place on the planet—the kind of sugary treats I was fed, for example: Pineapple Lumps and Hokey Pokey ice cream. Just like Australia's Vegemite and the crocodile tail I ate in Sydney, they were all added to my list of things I never thought I would ever eat.

But the biggest surprise came when James told me that he would drive me to the set of *The Hobbit*! After a long drive through the undulating green hills of the North Island, we arrived at the small, sleepy town of Matamata. From there, a small van took us over an unpaved country road to the farmland that Peter Jackson rented to shoot his movies. When we walked up to the set, our guide explained that the entire area was still used by the local farmer for his sheep. The Hobbit holes in the side of the hills looked as if they had been there forever. Gardeners had started to plant new fruit trees, flowers, and plants to allow them to grow naturally until the filming for *The Hobbit* began.

"It isn't hard to imagine why both Bilbo and Frodo didn't really want to leave the Shire for an adventure," I said in the microphone of my recorder. I couldn't pass up the chance of recording a podcast and to share this unexpected visit to Middle-earth with my listeners. "Everything you see in the movies is still here! Bag End, the small river that is supposed to connect to the Brandywine River, the big Party Tree, the roads that lead to Tuckborough and to Bree. Middle-earth has never seemed so real to me!"

I had been an avid reader of J.R.R. Tolkien's books since high school. I first discovered *The Hobbit*, followed by *The Lord of the Rings* trilogy. Tolkien was a devout, lifelong Catholic. Even though religion seems to be completely absent from the world of Middle-earth he created, Tolkien's books are nevertheless imbued with a Catholic worldview. What fascinated me about Tolkien's work was that he was able to speak about sin, grace, and redemption by incorporating these elements in the story without going the easy route of turning the entire thing into a series of metaphors, like C.S. Lewis did in *The Chronicles of Narnia*. Tolkien was much more subtle. Despite the beauty of the Shire, Middle-earth is a broken world. Similar to the way the fall of the angels preceded the fall of Adam and Eve, Melkor, an angelic being, rebelled against Ilúvatar, the creator of Middle-earth. Now called Morgoth, his fall to darkness leads others to follow in his footsteps, like Sauron, the main villain in *The Lord of the Rings*. Many other creatures in Middle-earth gave in to hatred and fear and became deformed servants of evil as a result. The One Ring symbolizes the temptation to use power for selfish needs, regardless of the consequences. All the protagonists in the story at one point have to choose which path to take. In the end, it's the path of virtue, self-sacrifice, and mercy that brings about redemption and true freedom.

These are wonderful themes for a series of Catholic programs. But how could I make a series of recordings about Tolkien's world that would appeal to a larger audience than just the community of Middle-earth scholars? I came up with two ideas. Once *The Hobbit* movies got the green light, I started to do a weekly podcast that covered the latest news about the production, similar to the way I had reported on the *Star Wars* prequels many years before. Two other Tolkien fans, Dave and Inge, added their expertise to the show, and soon, our program was firmly established in the world of *Hobbit* fandom. The combination of movie news and deeper discussions about the universe Tolkien had created attracted a large audience that kept growing over time, especially after Peter Jackson announced that he would make no fewer than three movies based on *The Hobbit*. Somehow, though, I kept thinking back to my experience in New Zealand. Being able to hear the sounds of the *Hobbit* set—the birds, the sheep in the distance, and the wind in the trees—added so much atmosphere to the recordings. How could I recreate that at home?

In 2007, in the wake of Jackson's *Lord of the Rings* movies, gaming company Turbine released a video game called *Lord of the Rings Online*. It was a game in the MMORPG genre, which stands for Massively Multiplayer Online Role-Playing Game. The best-known example in this genre was *World of Warcraft*, and *Lord of the Rings Online* offered players similar gameplay within a virtually recreated Middle-earth. The game allowed a player to walk around as an elf, a dwarf, a human, or a Hobbit and complete quests in areas that closely matched the descriptions in

Tolkien's books. The game had beautiful, lush graphics, and very realistic sound. You could hear your footsteps in the grass, the sounds and the chatter in the streets of Bree, and the growling of orcs and goblins in the more dangerous areas of Middle-earth. In short, it was the perfect audio environment for a podcast!

One day, I started to travel around Middle-earth with a few other Tolkien experts, talking about the stories and the themes of *The Hobbit* and *The Lord of the Rings* while actually visiting the places from the books and the movies! The element of discovery, the atmospheric sounds, and the expertise of my cohosts resulted in an adventurous show that appealed to fans of both the books and the movies. In addition to that, it also proved to be very popular with the large, worldwide community of gamers! Every time new areas were added to the game, we would gather our virtual fellowship and head out the door on our digital horses to explore new regions in Middle-earth.

The series, *Secrets of Middle-earth*, also revealed another advantage of new-media productions: They continue to attract an audience over the years! In television or radio, a lot of resources are spent on programs that air only once. But our download statistics show that certain episodes of our Middle-earth show have continued to be listened to years after they were recorded. This phenomenon is also called the long tail of new media products. A show that had taken only a couple hours to prepare and sixty minutes to record could be downloaded tens of thousands of times over the years. This is one of the reasons I continue to encourage the Catholic Church to invest in new media productions. Blogs, ebooks, podcasts, and videos usually require a modest investment, but the efficiency and reach of these programs far surpasses anything in traditional publishing, radio, and television. It is like lembas, the elven bread given to Sam and Frodo: A very small piece of it can feed you for days. Similarly, a very small investment of time and effort can lead to productions that not only last for months or years but also can feed a multitude of people from all over the world.

Let me give you another example of how a small investment of time and money can lead to the creation of a series of programs that reaches a huge global audience: my series about the *Secrets of Angels and Demons*.

Angels and Demons

"Fr. Roderick, *quel sorpresa*, what a surprise! What brings you here?"

I looked up from my table at the cantina of the Gregorian University where I was reading a book and sipping a nice cappuccino, the kind you can find only in Rome. An older priest walked toward me. I recognized him right away; he worked at the Vatican, and I had met him several times while I was studying social communications at this same university. He spotted the book I was reading and frowned.

"*Angels and Demons* by Dan Brown? I don't have to tell you that this author made everything up, right? There are more factual errors in that book than there are tourists at the Trevi Fountain!"

"I know; I'm here to record an audio series about the real stories behind the places and events mentioned in the book. I'm preparing my notes for my recordings later today."

"Ah, excellent! It won't hurt for people to get a different take on what they read about the Vatican in books like that," he said, smiling. "Well, I won't keep you from your work; it is good to see you again!"

Half an hour later, I was walking down the streets of Rome to my first recording location: St. Peter's Square. I had arrived the day before on a budget flight from Holland that had cost me as little as twenty euro. My goal? To record a series to separate facts from fiction in the movie *Angels and Demons* based on Dan Brown's bestseller with the same title. Dan Brown wrote the book before his breakthrough novel, *The Da Vinci Code*, but the movie was presented as a sequel. I heard that Dan Brown was actually in Rome right then for the European premiere that week. I had seen the movie the night before, and I planned on following in the footsteps of the main character of the book, Robert Langdon, visiting the same locations that were mentioned in the book. I went from St. Peter's Square to the Pantheon, from there to the Piazza del Popolo, the Church of Santa Maria della Vittoria, the Piazza Navona, and finally the famous Passetto, the secret papal escape route between the Vatican and Castel Sant'Angelo.

At each location, I hoped to record background information about the things Dan Brown got right and the things he made up. One problem: My flight home was scheduled for the next morning. I had exactly one day to record the entire series—twelve episodes of about an hour each. It was going to be a long day!

That day, I worked nonstop until almost midnight. But I loved doing this work. I felt like an explorer—or a documentary film-maker trying to convey information in the form of a story. It was almost like a radio play with the sounds of the city surrounding the listener. I knew that a series recorded on location in Rome would be much more appealing to a potential audience than anything I could record at home in my small studio. The trick was to take listeners along on a journey of discovery, to make them feel as if they were there. As usual, I received some strange looks from bystanders while talking into my small digital recorder, but I had been doing this for years, so I was used to it. The only location that could potentially pose problems was St. Peter's Square.

"Sir, can I ask you what you are doing?" A security agent walked toward me, barely two minutes after I started recording on St. Peter's Square. In *Angels and Demons*, Robert Langdon discovers intriguing symbols on white tiles surrounding the obelisk in the middle of the square, and I was staring at the exact tile mentioned in the book, ready to explain to my future listeners that they weren't part of some intricate conspiracy.

The guard pointed at my recorder. "Are you a journalist? It is not allowed to do reporting here without a permit."

This had happened to me before, and it had always bothered me. Plenty of tourists could walk around filming every pigeon and every stone of the square, but as soon as someone is walking around talking into something that is not a phone, it seemed that everybody gets a Code Red and receives instructions to investigate this suspicious activity. Of course I knew that the Vatican was its own country and could enforce its own rules, but this still felt like a public space. Even if I had been a reporter, why wasn't I allowed to make an audio recording here? What were they afraid of?

But I couldn't afford to start a fundamental discussion about the freedom of the press with this security agent, so I told him that I was not a journalist but just recording some audio impressions for some friends that couldn't be here with me. Which, strictly speaking, was true: I consider my listeners to be friends, albeit connected via digital media, and I was recording audio impressions. My reply in combination with my priestly attire seemed to reassure the guard; he walked away, and I resumed my recording. I was almost finished. It was getting late, and I had to get back in time for some sleep because my plane was leaving early the next day.

When I sat down on the side of my bed that evening to say a prayer before going to sleep, I suddenly realized how tired I was. My feet hurt from running all over Rome. But my mission was accomplished: I had been able to produce twelve episodes on an absolute shoestring budget in record time. This could very well be the way of the future—producing shows with limited resources and time as efficiently as possible. But there was something vital I still had to do: find an audience for these programs.

Back home, I spent some time editing the episodes, adding snippets from the movie trailer of *Angels and Demons* to evoke the atmosphere of the movie, and then I posted the show online. The resulting exposure was incredible. Apple's iTunes Store picked it up and promoted it on their main pages. The result? More than sixty thousand downloads per episode in a very short time. And even today, new people are finding the series online, and I still get e-mail from new listeners, demonstrating once more the long-tail effect of new media.

For a lot of people, the Church's culture and modern popular culture seem like two opposite sides of a river. But just like the bridges that were built to cross the Tiber, it is important that the Church keeps building new bridges in modern media.

The Return of Star Wars

The summer before I moved to Rome for my studies in social communications, I visited the area of Lake Como in northern Italy. It was partly to learn a bit of Italian, but also because I had heard that George Lucas had been filming there for his second *Star Wars* prequel, *Attack of the Clones.* According to the rumors on the Internet, the film crew had spent several days filming at the beautiful Villa del Balbianello. The place looked as if it came straight out of a fairy tale, beautifully located at the foot of a crystal-clear lake.

As you can imagine, I was trying to figure out the plot of the next *Star Wars* movie, so I walked around the villa trying to picture what they might have filmed there. I started a casual conversation with a young woman who worked there as a tourist guide. At first, she was hesitant to say anything about the movie, claiming that she had signed a nondisclosure contract, but after a while, she did reveal a couple of details. Actors Hayden Christensen and Natalie Portman had been there, and in addition to some romantic scenes on the balcony near the lake, they also filmed a scene on a nearby hill with a beautiful view of the surrounding area. She told me how I could get there, but she warned me that I would probably have to climb over some fences in order to reach the place.

I felt like a detective as I crouched under the barbed wire that surrounded the meadow on top of the small hill. The woman was right: The view was amazing. It made me think of the meadow at the start of *The Sound of Music.* It was definitely a nice setting for a romantic encounter. On my way back, I talked to an old man who had witnessed the filming from afar. He pointed his walking stick to the hill I had just come from. "They were just running around in the grass like two youngsters. I have no idea what movie they were part of. But there sure were a lot of Americans walking around here that day!"

I remember how amazed I was when I recognized the same meadow during the premiere of the actual movie. Thanks to special effects, the hill was now surrounded by spectacular waterfalls, and huge, cow-like alien creatures were grazing in the background while Padmé and Anakin ran around in the grass, madly in love. The beautiful eighteenth-century Italian villa I had visited was now part of the *Star Wars* universe; it featured in the movie as a lake resort on the planet of Naboo, where Anakin Skywalker had taken refuge with Padmé Amidala after a failed assassination attempt on the planet of Coruscant.

I never thought that I would ever return to the world of *Star Wars*. After all, the saga was complete. Six movies was all we would get. And yet, once more, there was an unexpected tremor in the Force that would allow me to reconnect with Wookiees, Jedi, and Ewoks from galaxies far, far away.

In October 2012, George Lucas announced that he had sold the *Star Wars* franchise to the Walt Disney Company for $4.05 billion. In the same announcement, we heard that Disney would produce three new *Star Wars* films, with the first one planned for release in 2015.

This, of course, presented me with another huge opportunity to return to the world of *Star Wars* and try to shed light on the new stories from a Catholic perspective. Thanks to social networks and SQPN, I had discovered quite a few very knowledgeable Catholic *Star Wars* fans, so assembling a panel of experts to produce a new series called *The Secrets of Star Wars* wouldn't be much of a problem!

It is funny to see how, after all these years, the circle seems to be complete. I started my adventures in new media with *Star Wars*, and now, many years later and much more experienced when it comes to the creation of audio and video programs, I am once again back in that universe far, far away.

And since we are talking about circles that are complete, there was another event that brought me back to the earliest adventures in new media: the election of a new pope!

CHAPTER SEVEN

Reach for the Sky

Back to the Future

On the day that Pope Benedict XVI surprised the world by announcing his resignation, lightning struck the dome of St. Peter's Basilica. The moment was captured on film. It reminded me of the scene in the first *Back to the Future* movie, when Marty McFly uses the 1.21 gigawatts generated by the lightning bolt that strikes the clock tower of Hill Valley to transport him back to the future. When I looked around at the crowd on St. Peter's Square, I felt like I had just stepped out of a DeLorean that had traveled through time. I was standing in the same spot as eight years ago. In front of the same basilica. Staring at the same chimney on top of the Sistine Chapel. Even holding a digital recorder in my hand to record what happened, just like in 2005. But this wasn't 2005. This was 2013. The future had become the present.

Heavy rain was pouring down from the sky. I clenched my teeth while trying to hold both my flimsy folding umbrella and my digital recorder in one hand, and a small video camera in the other. My hand was cramping. I had been standing there for several hours now, and the crowd around me was getting bigger and bigger. A Franciscan friar in brown robes was texting something with his cellphone and didn't notice that a splash of water from his black umbrella almost hit my recorder.

"*Attenzione!*" I said, while jumping away, trying to protect my electronic equipment.

"*Scusi, Padre!*" he apologized when he saw my terrified look.

I couldn't afford an equipment failure or a short circuit. Not today! From under my umbrella, I looked at the tiny chimney on the right. The day before, on the first evening of the conclave, thick, black smoke had indicated that the cardinals hadn't been able to find a new pope yet. The same thing had happened at the end of the morning session, only a few hours ago. And yet, something told me that this day would be the day. Just like in 2005, I was determined to be there when it happened. This time, I wanted to capture *everything*—not just in audio form but with video as well. But unless the rain stopped and I could get rid of my umbrella, this seemed like a mission impossible.

What a contrast to my work in radio and television! Only two weeks earlier, I had been surrounded by a camera crew, a director, and a producer while reporting on the final day of Pope Benedict XVI's pontificate. At 7:30 P.M., I stood in front of a camera on a hill on the left side of the Vatican, ready to report live via satellite on Dutch national TV. With the basilica in the background, I tried to convey the mood in Rome now that we were saying farewell to this gentle, modest pope from Germany who had made his startling announcement on February 11. The technician had given me an earpiece through which I could hear the voices of the studio hosts in the Netherlands. In the corner of my eye, I could see two other reporters standing, just like me, in front of bright spotlights, a monitor, and a camera. It felt good to be surrounded by all these professionals who took care of all the technical and directorial aspects. The only thing I had to do was to look at the camera and talk.

I had done this once before, years ago. It had been a very intimidating experience. Like most people, I had no idea how complicated it was to establish a live video connection between two places. Most people naively assume that the person in front of the camera is able to see the hosts in the studio, just as they can see him or her. In reality, when you're in front of the camera, you don't see anything. The studio lights are blindingly bright, and the only thing in front of you is the dark, circular lens of the television camera. There is an audio lag of several seconds as well. And yet, you have to somehow pretend that you are making eye contact with the viewers at home, having a normal conversation even though your surroundings are anything but normal.

This time, fortunately, I had several years of television experience under my belt. A couple of years ago, I had been asked to become the host of a weekly Catholic program on national TV, so I had grown used to staring into a camera, mentally visualizing the people I was talking to. It's something that has become second nature ever since I started podcasting. I try to act as if the people in my audience are there with me. Even when I know that millions of people might be watching at the same time, I still try to visualize that one person or family sitting in front of their TV. "It's never you versus a crowd," my radio teacher at the Gregorian University had said. "Communication happens between you and your listener. Approach it as a personal, one-on-one conversation. Talk as if you were talking to a friend."

The Heart of Social Media

It's that same personal connection that forms the heart of the success of social media. Ever since my arrival in Rome, I had been posting photos and video clips of my activities on Facebook and

Twitter. Whether I was reporting on the black smoke or posting a picture of a delicious Italian ice cream, I knew that many friends from all over the world were sharing in the experience, reposting and sharing my reports with thousands of others.

And thanks to that same social media, I quickly discovered that many of the friends I had made in Catholic media over the years were with me in Rome! Lino Rulli and Fr. Dave Dwyer, for instance, who wanted to interview me on their daily radio show for the Catholic Channel. Or Scot Landry from the Archdiocese of Boston, who was using his iPhone to post video reports to YouTube. My friends from Australia were also there: Kerry Myers from the *Catholic Weekly* and Katrina Lee from the Archdiocese of Sydney. When I covered the conclave in 2005, I was alone. I sensed the potential of new media to reach out and connect with people, but none of it had materialized yet.

Eight years later, despite the cold rain pouring from the skies on St. Peter's Square, I felt a heartwarming wave of emotion and gratitude as I realized how much this global community of friends meant to me.

And that's when it happened. Smoke started to rise from the chimney. It was white! We had a new pope! Almost simultaneously, the rain stopped falling. Without the sea of umbrellas, I could get a good view of the smoke and the large bells of the basilica that confirmed the news. "*Habemus Papam*!" announced French Cardinal Tauran, and the crowd responded with a roaring applause that almost drowned the rest of the announcement. "It's Cardinal Bergoglio!" a priest next to me exclaimed while I pointed my camera at him. "And he chose the name of Francis!"

In the video I made that night, I tried to capture the roller coaster of emotions the crowd went through—from the initial surprise to the wild enthusiasm at the first appearance of Pope Francis to the deep, reverent silence when he asked for our prayers. Even now, when I watch that video, I feel the same emotion I felt back then. The thing is, I would probably have never been able to make a video like this in the traditional way. There is a sense of immediacy that you don't get when you move around with a full-blown camera crew. The video was viewed thousands of times via Facebook and YouTube, and my broadcast colleagues liked it so much that they showed it several times on Dutch TV.

The experience opened a world of possibilities. Just as minia-ture audio equipment revolutionized the world of radio through podcasting, small cameras and guerrilla-style video production are turning the world of television upside down. Not just because of the technological advances and diminishing costs of the equip-ment, but because of the new style of media made possible by these small, low-cost devices. Media that is personal, authentic, and relatable because it isn't produced by big anonymous compa-nies, but by people you can call your friends.

Don't get me wrong: There will always be a place for traditional, big media geared for mass audiences. The advent of blogs didn't mean the end of books, the success of podcasting didn't make radio obsolete, and no matter how many thousands of videos are uploaded to the Web every minute, there will still be people watching TV and going to the movies. But new media can reach audiences at a deeper, personal, and even spiritual level. And that is why they are so important for the Church.

Seven Things Pope Francis Taught Me

Pope Francis has already proved to be a great communicator. His words and attitude have touched people right from the start of his pontificate. Here are seven things he taught me about media and about communication:

1. It's not about you. In his first audience with media representatives a few days after his election, I vividly remember how Pope Francis emphasized that we are called not to communicate ourselves, but to express truth, goodness, and beauty. "In person!" the pope added. We are not the center of the world. Christ is. He is the heart of the Church.

2. Be humble. From day one, I was impressed by Pope Francis's humble attitude. The same humility marked his predecessors. True humility comes from the knowledge that we are here to serve one another. Jesus told his apostles that he came not to be served but to serve. It is something I have to ask myself time and again when I look in the bathroom mirror at the start of a new day. *How can I help? How can I serve my brothers and sisters today through my work in new media?*

3. Don't forget the poor. The pope told us that first day how he decided to choose the name Francis. When it became clear that the majority of the cardinals had chosen him to be the next pope, Cardinal Hummes embraced him and said: "Don't forget the poor!" And that is when the name Francis of Assisi came into his heart. This concern for the simple, the humble, the poor, the forgotten, those who do not matter in the eyes of the world touched me. *Are my eyes seeing the needs of the people around me? Do I notice the struggles of those I encounter online and in the world?*

4. Never despair. The Catholic Church has gone through difficult times over the past years. In his final audience, Pope Benedict XVI mentioned how he sometimes felt like St. Peter with the apostles in the boat on the Sea of Galilee when the seas were rough and the wind against them. And yet, he said, Christ is always in the boat and he will not let her sink. Just like many others, I have had my share of nasty comments on the Internet, and more than once, I was the target of derision in interviews simply because I was a priest. It sometimes seems impossible to repair the bridge between the Church and the world. But in his homily on Palm Sunday, Pope Francis admonished us to never give way to discouragement. Our hope is founded on the knowledge that Jesus carries us on his shoulders.

5. Don't pursue what you don't need. In his address to the media, Pope Francis told us how much he would like a Church which is both poor and for the poor. Before he became pope, he was known for his simple lifestyle, using public transportation and cooking his own meals. His example has made me reevaluate my own priorities. *How many news feeds do I really need to follow? Do I really need all those games, movies, and TV series? Am I spending my money on superfluous gadgets or can I be happy with last year's technology?* Tough questions for a geek like me. But I need to think about them.

6. Protect others in friendship. During his installation Mass, Pope Francis reflected upon the example of St. Joseph, whose feast it was that day. Like him, the pope said, we are called to be protectors of those around us and of God's creation. This struck a chord with me. The world of media can be harsh, impersonal, and relentless.

I sometimes pale when I see what people—often under the guise of anonymity—say or write. Many children and teens suffer from bullying, a problem that has also spread to the Internet. I think it's my inner Jedi that feels the call to action. I can use my presence in new media to create a climate of respect and friendship—first by avoiding anger and harshness in my own behavior.

7. Reach out to the world and reach for the sky. One of the first things Pope Francis mentioned on the balcony of St. Peter's Basilica was evangelization. Later, on Palm Sunday, he invited the youth to go to the ends of the world with Jesus's message. And he pointed to the Virgin Mary, the Star of Evangelization. I love this. It is a movement that embraces the world and reaches for the sky. Like a guiding star, Mary points us the way to her Son. And like the Magi, anyone is invited to join this communal journey of faith and friendship.

Including Jedi, geeks, and Hobbits. Including you.

So what are you waiting for?

ABOUT THE AUTHOR

Fr. Roderick Vonhögen studied social communications in Rome and has traveled the world to initiate countless Catholic new media projects focused on education and evangelization. A producer, blogger, speaker, and media host, Fr. Roderick is the founder and CEO of Star Quest Production Network (SQPN), a multimedia organization that uses the media for religious information, evangelization, catechesis, formation, and education.